ABSOLUTE POWER

THE SCREENPLAY

BY

WILLIAM GOLDMAN

BASED ON THE BEST-SELLING NOVEL BY
DAVID BALDACCI

CASTLE ROCK ENTERTAINMENT PRESENTS A MALPASO PRODUCTION CLINT EASTWOOD GENE HACKMAN ED HARRIS "ABSOLUTE POWER"
MUSIC BY LENNIE NIEHAUS EDITED BY JOEL COX PRODUCTION DESIGNED BY HENRY BUMSTEAD DIRECTOR OF PHOTOGRAPHY JACK N. GREEN, A.S.C. EXECUTIVE PRODUCER TOM ROOKER
PRODUCED BY KAREN SPIEGEL BASED ON THE NOVEL BY DAVID BALDACCI SCREENPLAY BY WILLIAM GOLDMAN PRODUCED AND DIRECTED BY CLINT EASTWOOD READ THE WARNER PAPERBACK COLUMBIA PICTURES

APPLAUSE
NEW YORK • LONDON

ABSOLUTE POWER by William Goldman

The author and publisher gratefully acknowledge the generous cooperation of Warner Books, Castle Rock Entertainment and David Baldacci in the publication of this screenplay.

Photos: Graham Kuhn

Library of Congress Cataloging-in-Publication Data

LC Catalog # 97–070279

British Library Cataloging-in-Publication Data

A catalogue record for this book is available from the British Library

ISBN: 1-55783-275-7

APPLAUSE BOOKS
211 West 71st Street
New York, NY 10023
Phone: (212) 496-7511
Fax: (212) 721-2856

A&C Black
Howard Road
Huntington, Cambs PE19 3EZ
Phone: 0171-242 0946
Fax: 0171-831-8478

10   9   8   7   6   5   4   3   2   1

Introduction

Absolute Power is the hardest screenplay I have ever written.

Eventually, it stopped me cold — for the first time I was faced with an assignment that I simply could not complete. And would never have been able to had Tony Gilroy not come in to save me.

THE NOVEL

November '94.

Martin Shafer who runs Castle Rock films called and said he was sending me *Executive Power*, a first novel by a young Washington lawyer, David Baldacci. Shafer mentioned nothing specific pertaining to the plot but he did tell me this: that Baldacci, in the last three weeks, had sold the worldwide book and movie rights for *five million dollars*.

Even in today's crazed scramble for material, a tad unusual.

The next day a 466 page typed manuscript arrived.

Curious as hell, I began turning pages.

Chapter 1, pages 3–17

A great old thief, **LUTHER WHITNEY**, breaks into a deserted mansion belonging to 80 year old **WALTER SULLIVAN**, one of the more powerful billionaires around. It is very tricky and tense, the break-in, pitting sophisticated burglary tools against a top of the line security system.

LUTHER makes his way to the master bedroom, takes what looks like a VCR remote from a nearby table, points it at what looks like an ordinary mirror, and clicks. The mirror swings open to reveal a room-sized vault —

— a vault with a chair in it, a chair facing the door.

LUTHER enters and starts bagging the goodies — cash, jewelry, coins, bonds, stamps, millions of dollars worth.

During this, a limo and a van are approaching the mansion. In the limo are two women and a man. One of the women is trying to undress the man, who is good-naturedly trying to fend her off. Both are drunk.

The other woman sits opposite watching with some distaste and dealing with a large appointment book.

LUTHER hears the cars, realizes he is in trouble because it's too late to escape. So he hides in the vault, shuts the door, sits in the chair.

Footsteps come closer and closer and the bedroom light is turned on and **LUTHER** is shocked and blinded and for a moment he thinks he's been found out. Then he realizes this: *it's a one-way mirror*. From the bedroom, it's just a mirror. But from where he sits, it's as if the mirror has disappeared — he has a life-sized view of what's happening in the bedroom just a few feet beyond —

— and what's happening is this: two very drunk people are clearly going to fuck . . .

LUTHER recognizes the two people: **THE WOMAN** is the 25 year old **CHRISTY SULLIVAN**, wife of **WALTER SULLIVAN**, the ancient billionaire. **THE MAN** is clearly not her husband — and **LUTHER** is stunned when he realizes who he is . . .

Pretty terrific start.

I had no idea where the story was going, but I knew I wasn't about to stop reading. I also had no idea who the main characters would be, but I guessed the trio would be around:

LUTHER WHITNEY, the great old thief.
CHRISTY SULLIVAN, the philandering blonde.
THE WELL DRESSED MAN who she was philandering with.

A total of three.

One thing to note here: movies are not Chekhov. You have

your star part, that's essential. And depending on what kind of flick it is, you have your love interest or your villain.

But you cannot have even half a dozen main characters. *The Big Chill*, sure. *Peter's Friends, Return of the Secaucus Seven.* But the glory days of the all-star cast MGM movie is (because of budget primarily) as removed as the ice age.

Chapter 2, pages 18–26

That same night, **JACK GRAHAM**, an attractive athletic young Washington attorney returns home from a fancy party. **JACK** has pretty much everything going for him, but be careful what you wish for, you might get it.

JACK is engaged to **JENNIFER BALDWIN**, who is gorgeous and the heiress to the Baldwin fortune, run by her father, **RANSOME BALDWIN**. **JACK** has a job at one of the top Washington law firms, which also handles the **BALDWIN** interests. **JACK** is new there, having taken the job at **JENNIFER'S** urging and because of his connection with the Baldwins, he will become a partner at the next review.

JACK goes to bed where he takes down a picture of his former fiance, **KATE WHITNEY**. They have not seen each other in four years but he knows she is now a State's Attorney. **JACK** loved **KATE**, still misses her, but misses her father **LUTHER**, with whom he was very close, almost as much.

JACK decides to call **KATE**, dials her, then hangs up after the beep sound as he loses his nerve.

Short, helpful, very tense — because while you are reading, what you are thinking is this: *get back to the bedroom.* There were also several new characters I knew I would be meeting again.

JACK GRAHAM; pretty clearly to be the hero.
KATE WHITNEY, even though she hasn't done much yet.
JENNIFER BALDWIN, the rich and beautiful fiancee.
Along with, please remember —
LUTHER WHITNEY, the great old thief.

CHRISTY SULLIVAN, the philandering blonde.
THE WELL DRESSED MAN who she was philandering with.

Bringing the total to six.
Six *major* characters.
So far.

Chapter 3 pages 27–57

Back to the vault. **LUTHER**, helpless, watches as the sex begins, heats up, gets violent, gets bloody. **THE MAN** tries to strangle **CHRISTY** but she slashes him in the arm with a letter opener and is about to stab him in the heart when he screams and **TWO WELL-DRESSED MEN** race in and blow her brains out.

At the same time, **KATE WHITNEY** is working late in her office. She thinks momentarily of her hated father, calls her home for messages but there is only a breather who hangs up. She goes back to work watched by a photo of herself and her mother from which **LUTHER** has been unmistakably ripped away.

Back in the bedroom, the naked and bleeding **ALAN RICHMOND, THE PRESIDENT OF THE UNITED STATES** is staring dumbly at the bloody letter opener in his hand that almost killed him. **BILL BURTON**, the older of the two Secret Service men who did the shooting is almost sick at the sight of blood and brains. His partner, **TIM COLLIN**, steadies him. **PRESIDENT RICHMOND** passes out as Chief of Staff **GLORIA RUSSELL** the other woman in the limousine, races in.

COLLIN reports the facts to **RUSSELL**. **RUSSELL** plans a cover-up. The room is sanitized and they all leave. But unknown to **RUSSELL** the letter opener which she commandeered has fallen from her purse behind the bed.

THE PRESIDENT, RUSSELL,BURTON, and **COLLIN** hurry down to the waiting cars, preparing to get the hell gone —

— which is when **RUSSELL** realizes the letter opener isn't in her purse.

LUTHER, who has left the vault, has taken it with him as he uncoils a rope and goes out the window.

THE SECRET SERVICE chase him on foot, almost catch him in a thrilling footrace, but he manages to make it to his car and zooms off.

RUSSELL, **BURTON** and **COLLIN** return to the bedroom, realize two facts, neither good for the Jews: (1) the letter opener is gone, complete with fingerprints of both the **PRESIDENT** and the murdered **CHRISTY SULLIVAN** on it (2) there also was an *eyewitness*.

They know they are in very deep shit indeed. And will be until they have murdered the eyewitness and have the letter opener back.

LUTHER knows the power of his enemies — he returns to his home, packs, flees into the night.

It was clear at this point why five million dollars had been spent. I thought it was just about the best opening for a commercial novel I had ever read. It was also clear that I was not reading the book strictly for pleasure. Sure that's present and crucial —

— but I was also being asked to turn it into a movie. And clearly, it was not going to be easy money at the brick factory.

More new characters who weren't leaving soon:
GLORIA RUSSELL, the Chief of Staff
BILL BURTON, the veteran Secret Service guy
TIM COLLIN, the young hotshot.
And let us not forget
JACK GRAHAM; pretty clearly to be the hero.
KATE WHITNEY, even though she hasn't done much yet.
JENNIFER BALDWIN, the rich and beautiful fiancee.
Along with, please remember
LUTHER WHITNEY, the great old thief
CHRISTY SULLIVAN, the philandering blonde.

THE WELL DRESSED MAN now revealed as **PRESIDENT ALAN RICHMOND**, who she was philandering with.

Nine characters now. And counting. I finished the book and then did something I have never done before when offered an assignment — I read the whole thing again. And as I did, I became convinced that more and more characters were simply crucial to the story. Here are some of them:

SETH FRANK, the detective trying to solve it all. *Maybe the lead.*

WANDA BROOME, who conceived the break-in with **LUTHER**.

WALTER SULLIVAN, the good billionaire and wronged husband.

SANDY LORD, SULLIVAN'S lawyer and a power in Washington.

LAURA SIMON, SETH'S top aide, who ties **LUTHER** to the crime.

MR. FLANDERS, a bystander who televised **LUTHER'S** murder.

MICHAEL MCCARTY, world's top assassin, hired to kill **LUTHER**.

And, just in case you went to the kitchen for a snack —

GLORIA RUSSELL, the Chief of Staff

BILL BURTON, the veteran Secret Service guy.

TIM COLLIN, the young hotshot.

And let us not forget —

JACK GRAHAM; pretty clearly to be the hero

KATE WHITNEY, even though she hasn't done much yet.

JENNIFER BALDWIN, the rich and beautiful fiancee.

Along with, please remember —

LUTHER WHITNEY, the great old thief

CHRISTY SULLIVAN, the philandering blonde.

THE WELL DRESSED MAN, now revealed as **PRESIDENT ALAN RICHMOND**, who she was philandering with.

You add it up, it's too horrible.

I could go on but that's more than enough to indicate the morass I was thinking about entering — you simply cannot have that many characters in a movie today. It's confusing, it's a turn-off, it's just *wrong*.

And wrong more than ever now, when the hunger for a vehicle role, a locomotive (as they sometimes refer to the male lead Out There) has reached hysterical heights.

My problem doctor was simply this: *There was no star part.*

LUTHER was the best character but he could not be the star, for many reasons, chiefly this: in a great shocker, he is murdered half-way through by orders of the President.

No to **LUTHER**.

JACK GRAHAM, the young lawyer was maybe the biggest part. But he didn't come into the story til very late, and the star must enter early.

No to **JACK GRAHAM**.

SETH FRANK was the cop on the trail. But he didn't solve that much. Couldn't be **SETH FRANK**.

What's a mother to do . . . ?

I called Shafer and said I would like to try it and I would try to write ten good roles— because that was what the material called for. Shafer said this: "It's OK. We'll go with ten one million dollar actors rather than one ten million dollar one."

All I had to do now was write the bastard.

Why did I say yes? Because I had not done a flat-out thriller since *Marathon Man*, was anxious to try another. Because it was Castle Rock, the best movie studio for writers in my third of a century in the business.

And because Baldacci (bless him) had written three sensational sequences. The opening seventy page rough sex with the President of the United States; the double assassination attempt to kill Luther, with both **COLLIN AND MCCARTY** having point blank shots at the old guy and, maybe most moving of all,

LUTHER'S shocking murder by COLLIN, which comes at a time when the reader thinks LUTHER is finally safe.

Wonderful stuff.

These three, I felt, were so strong they would support the remainder of the screenplay, no matter how badly I might screw things up.

Aside to young screenwriters: no, I am not shitkicking when I say this last. I am always terrified I am going to screw everything up. The most hideous advice — and at the same time the most releasing — was given to me by George Roy Hill, still and always the greatest director I ever worked with. I had just taken on the job of trying to make the famous Woodward Bernstein Watergate book somehow translate to screen. Hill, a world-class sadist, looked at me, and these were his words: "*All the President's Men?* Everybody's going to be waiting for that one." And here he smiled. "Don't fuck it up."

I recently ran into Ben Stiller at a Knicks game; who has his own demons trying to figure out *What Makes Sammy Run?* "Don't fuck it up" I told him.

He kind of smiled...

THE FIRST DRAFT

May, 1995.

I called this draft *Not the Executive Power*, because I thought Baldacci's title so damaging — there were already several other moves ahead of us in the pipeline that also were called 'Executive' something or other. Even more important, at least to me was this: I kept forgetting the name of the novel when people asked me what I was working on.

The first draft script ran 145 pages — too long, I knew that but I also knew that the crucial thing for me in this initial pass was to get the story written. And then read it.

I got it written.

I read it.

Ugh.

It looked like a screenplay; if you lifted it up, it hoisted like a screenplay.

But it just kind of lay there.

No one to really root for—

—except old Luther who died halfway through.

Not having someone to root for is a terrible problem.

But an even bigger one was this: the story didn't end, it just stopped.

Endings are just a bitch. (Tattoo that behind your eyelids.)

The best ending of mine I think is *Butch Cassidy*. And I like the 'as you wish' in *The Princess Bride*.

Endings in thrillers are particularly brutal. At least they have been for me. I've tried several — *Marathon Man*, I guess *No Way To Treat A Lady*, I guess *Magic*, I guess *Control*. If you read any of them, chances are if you remember them at all it's not for the way they concluded.

Maybe it's because the initial pulse for the story was played out before the ending came. *Marathon Man*, at least as I remember, came from two ideas: (1) What if someone in your family whom you had known and loved wasn't remotely what you had thought? (Babe — Dustin Hoffman in the movie,) has no idea his beloved brother Doc (Roy Scheider) is a spy and not a businessman. What if the world's most wanted Nazi had to come to Manhattan? Szell (Olivier, yesss) has to come here to retrieve his diamond fortune from a bank, first ascertaining was it safe for him to go there?

Well, by the time blood has been spilled, by the time Olivier has slaughtered Scheider and Hoffman has cornered Olivier it was just a matter of mixing and matching. I had nothing much more up my sleeve.

David Baldacci didn't have a sleeveful either. The manuscript I read ended like this: in the last chapter, SETH, the detective who's been in charge of the CHRISTY SULLIVAN murder case, comes to the White House along with a bunch of law enforcement officials and arrests PRESIDENT ALAN RICHMOND. RICHMOND says as President, legally he can't be served with anything. SETH replies that after his impeachment, he'll be plain ALAN RICHMOND again and when that happens he's going to trial.

Not heart pounding but solid enough.

The epilogue is the quagmire.

JACK has gone on a trip and come back to Washington and *knows nothing* of recent events, such as the murder trial of the President of the United States. 'Inconceivable,' as Vizzini used to say. SETH comes to visit him and fills JACK in on what's been happening. COLLIN got twenty years to life, GLORIA RUSSELL got 1,000 hours of community service, RICHMOND lied on the stand, was torn apart on cross, was found guilty and given the death penalty.

Clearly, I had to come up with an exciting ending. My brain chose this time to go on Holiday.

So did I, and on Christmas afternoon of 1994 I found myself walking around a polo field in Barbados with John and Alyce Cleese whining about my ending problem. One of them, I think it was Alyce, said, 'Why doesn't another woman kill him?'

Sometimes there's God so quickly.

Not the Executive Power ended this way: SETH the detective hero and JACK, the lawyer hero go to the White House and talk on the lawn with the President who denies everything and has letters (false but sworn to) backing up his case. He then explains why they can't touch him.

RICHMOND
Because no one wants you to —
(beat)
— we live in the age of celebrity — Michael Jordan could shoot
Mother Teresa on live TV and get a hung jury — people need
us, now, more than ever — the world is going so fast — people
are more frightened now than they've ever been — they don't
want to hear bad things about those they love —
(beat)
— and they love me. And you know they do.
*(He gestures for them to rise. They
start to walk)*
Think of the headlines, think of the hysteria.
(he looks at them)
Jack — Seth — you've got a case based on wisps of smoke. I've
got all the power in the world. Now think hard — how much do
you want this country to suffer?

SETH
(whispered)
Not that much.

JACK
(helplessly)
You mean he's gonna win?

CUT TO

RICHMOND. *The sweetest smile.*

RICHMOND
The good guys always do.
*(hold on his famous face a moment,
then —)*
CUT TO

And what we cut to was the exterior of another mansion.
Then inside, outside a door where COLLIN paced, RUSSELL
worked. A woman's cry comes from inside. They glance at each
other, go on as before. Another feminine cry. On as before.

Then the sound of gunfire from the bedroom.

COLLIN AND RUSSELL rush inside to see a naked drunk blonde with a gun who can't stop giggling. 'He dared me," she says.

RICHMOND lies beside her, shot in the heart.

CUT TO

A CEMETERY. We hear Bernard Shaw telling CNN viewers that **RICHMOND'S** sudden fatal heart attack has shocked the nation but we've been through worse and we'll come through this too.

We're at **LUTHER'S** grave now. **JACK AND KATE, LUTHER'S DAUGHTER,** pay their last respects to the old guy.

Final Fade out.

Stephen Sondheim once said this: "I cannot write a bad song. You begin it here, build, end there. The words will lay properly on the music so they can be sung, that kind of thing. You may hate it, but it will be a proper song."

I sometimes feel that way about my screenplays. I've been doing them for so long now and I've attempted most genres. I know about entering the story as late as possible, entering each scene as late as possible, that kind of thing. You may hate it, but it will be a proper screenplay.

This first draft was proper as hell — you just didn't give much of a shit.

I met with the Castle Rock people, Martin Shafer, Liz Glotzer and Andy Scheinman; Andy is Rob Reiner's producer and the best non-writer when it comes to discussing scripts I have ever met.

They still wanted to make *Absolute Power*. (By now, Baldacci had come up with the title.) They just didn't want to make this version of the story.

Couldn't I give us someone to root for, someone we could care about; in other words, was there somewhere in the material, please God, a star part? Because the movie needed it.

They agreed on that.

I agreed with them.

But the same problem still haunted me —

— *there was not now and had never been a star part.*

THE SECOND DRAFT

October 1995.

I must explain something about the way I work — I have always only done movies I wanted to do — which means caring for *and being faithful to, the source material.*

I had never changed a story this much.

If I could figure out how to do it at all.

I went over and over my three choices.

1) LUTHER

Still by far the best character in both the book and the movie. But he had to die. Not just because it provided a wonderful chance for a strong scene. Luther's death provided the impact the story needed to sustain itself. Morally and viscerally. Because he was the most decent person in the story in spite of his occupation.

Definitely could not be LUTHER.

2) JACK GRAHAM

The logical choice really. He ends up with the girl, LUTHER'S DAUGHTER KATE, so he carries that emotion with him. Also, he is close to LUTHER, in fact, he's the one LUTHER turns to when he decides to try and expose PRESIDENT RICHMOND.

Problem: That happens literally halfway through the novel (and on page 71 of the 145 page first draft)

Could I bring Jack in earlier?

Sure. This wasn't a documentary. I could do anything.

I could open the movie with Jack being born if I wanted to.

But if I did bring him in earlier he would have just stood there. Baldacci brings him in a lot sooner in the novel but essentially, JACK just deals with his own personal relationships which are OK for a book, which can meander, but a movie isn't like that.

So could I really bring JACK in earlier?

Not without totally changing everything and making it JACK'S movie — but it *couldn't* be, because JACK wasn't in the goddamn vault, and what was seen from the vault, and its consequences, *had* to be the story.

Definitely could not be JACK.

3) SETH FRANK. SETH, the detective trying to solve the murder, might seem like the most logical. Detectives are there from the uncovering of the crime, and move along til the solution.

But not here.

The crime itself is not only a high point of the whole story, it also takes thirty pages of the first draft. And and and — SETH doesn't do all that much. Jack solves his share too. Definitely could not be SETH.

A double hero would be best.

Problem: I'd already failed trying it that way.

"Sheesh" as Calvin used to tell us.

I went over them again and again.

LUTHER? No.

JACK? No.

SETH? No.

If you happened to be walking on the east side of Manhattan in the early fall of '95, that sound you heard was me screaming.

Finally, I remembered Mr. Abbott.

One of the great breaks of my non-book career came in 1960 when I was among those called in to doctor a musical in trouble, *Tenderloin*. The show eventually was not a success. But the experience was profound.

George Abbott, the legitimately legendary Broadway director was the director of the show — he was closing in on 75 during our months together and hotter than ever. (We are talking about one of those careers — if you are a sports fan, think of the Babe or Wilt.) He had made his Broadway acting debut in 1913. The first play he wrote appeared in 1925.

You've heard of this year's phenomenal musical hit, *Chicago*? Well, Mr. Abbott directed the original play in 1926. It opened in December of the year and was his *second* success within three months, since he also wrote and directed *Broadway*, which opened some ninety days earlier.

Mr. Abbott liked to keep busy.

He directed a bunch of movies too, but mainly he stayed close to New York. He was connected with more famous and successful shows than anyone else, as producer, director, writer, or star.

Then he turned sixty-five and really got going. *Pajama Game*, (also the movie) *Damn Yankees* (also the move) *Fiorello* (Pulitzer Prize).

Which was when we met.

Mr. Abbott was a big man, six-two maybe, ramrod straight, not warm or welcoming. Someone wrote of him: "If he's ever late, you figure there's been an accident." The most totally professional man that ever walked the earth. A lot of people were intimidated by him.

I was not remotely intimidated.

Try *terrified*.

And as I was going through my second draft madness, I remembered a Mr. Abbott story. He was backstage during rehearsals, and he crossed the stage into the auditorium because the actors were waiting for him in the lounge downstairs.

This was the dancers time to use the stage.

There were a dozen of them on stage now as he walked by. They were not dancing but just standing there, hands on jutted hips, waiting. The choreographer sat in the audience alone, his head in his hands. "What's going on?" Mr. Abbott asked him.

The choreographer looked at Mr. Abbott, shook his head. "I can't figure out what they should do next."

Mr. Abbott never stopped moving. (How could he when the actors were waiting for him?) He jumped the three feet from the stage to the aisle. "Well, have them do *something*, " Mr. Abbott said. "That way we'll have something to change."

He continued on up the aisle.

The choreographer got off his ass, started moving the dancers.

As I remembered Mr. Abbott I got off my ass too. We were not going to shoot the second draft I reminded myself. So just write something so we'll have something to change.

LUTHER could not be my guy for reasons of death.

JACK could have been — his love affair with LUTHER'S daughter made that appealing. Except for this: in the novel and in the first draft too, *LUTHER and KATE never once talked to each other*. She betrays him, arranges for his capture — but that moment when she serves as decoy is their only contact in the Baldacci story. (They are estranged and have been for years when the story begins, and after the murder LUTHER is terrified to ever talk to her, for fear the secret service might kill her on the theory that she might know something)

I didn't want to mess with that.

No to JACK.

So SETH, by elimination, became my star.

There was still the problem of his not solving all that much. But I figured I could help that by giving him stuff to do that had belonged to other characters in the novel and the first draft.

One of the ways I did this was by giving him a family. I have two daughters, Jenny and Susanna, who loved Nancy Drew when they were kids. Guess what ? — SETH now also had daughters with those names. Who were fifteen, had outgrown Nancy but not the notion of being detectives.

The family was a way to keep SETH around, and also to get rid of exposition that other characters carried earlier. And it made SETH vulnerable so, near the end, when he is closing in on RICHMOND, the President has BURTON AND COLLIN send him a message by instructing them to hurt his family. Which they do, driving them off the road, putting ELAINE and the TWINS into the hospital. So SETH has a huge emotional score to settle when in the last scene, he visits the White House and brings RICHMOND down.

Not Shakespearean, no. But maybe an improvement over the first draft. And SETH was now at the center of pretty much everything possible. I had certainly written a star part which was primarily what I meant to do.

I sent it out. Fingers very much crossed.

Because this draft was going to Clint Eastwood. His agent had called while I was writing this draft and indicated he wouldn't mind taking a look at this draft when it was done.

I was desperate to work with Eastwood, had been for decades. He is quietly having one of the very greatest careers. Along with John Wayne, the two most durable stars in history. Plus plus plus the directing.

Eastwood as SETH — set the blood racing.

I had given them *something*. So at last we had something to change.

Little did he know...

THIRD DRAFT

December, 1995.

The second draft got out to Castle Rock around the 20th of October. Their reaction was good — not terrific but certainly good — and they were very appreciative about the amount of work that had gone into changing it.

Now, nothing to do but wait for Eastwood.

On the first of November Martin Shafer called to report that Eastwood definitely was reading it.

Then he called later that day and this is what he said. Eastwood had already read it. He thought it was absolutely OK.

But —

— big but —

— he had already played guys like SETH and didn't want to play that character again —

— now Shafer dropped the shoe —

— EASTWOOD was interested in playing LUTHER. He thought LUTHER was a terrific character but —

— amazingly huge but —

—*Eastwood wanted LUTHER to live and to bring down the President.*

I was rocked.

During these days of waiting my fantasies of writing a movie for Clint Eastwood grew out of all control. I was even more desperate to work with him —

— I simply didn't know if I could write it.

I asked Shafer would Eastwood commit in advance? — I was terrified of changing it so totally — always assuming I could figure out how — only to have him say no.

The answer was he would not. He would have to read it first. (I knew that of course. I was just scared and floundering)

One other problem — it was now November, I was literally starting from scratch again and I knew this: *I had to get it in before Christmas.* His agent had indicated as much, because Eastwood, who had taken time off after *The Bridges of Madison County*, was ready to go to work again. After Christmas he would be gone to something else leaving me dead in the water.

I told Shafer I would have to let him know.

These were the words I wrote in my journal that night:

HOW, GOD?

I spent the next days trying to come up with anything at all that might spark me, give me the confidence (always the greatest need) to plunge ahead.

A few days later I wrote this thought down: "**LUTHER** could use his street contacts — beggars who work the streets — to find out where **CHRISTY SULLIVAN** spent the day before she was murdered."

Explanation — Baldacci is kind of vague on this, what **CHRISTY** did earlier that day of her tryst. I figured maybe I could think of something exciting, it would be a way **LUTHER** could get something incriminating on **RICHMOND**.

Snooze.

Andy Scheinman came in to spend a couple of days with me. We got some stuff but not a lot and none of it splendid.

On the 10th of November I told Andy one of three things would happen. (1) I figured out how to do it and wrote it or (2) I realize I couldn't write it and bowed out and they bring in someone fast to replace me, or (3) we bring in someone to outline it and I would consult on the script.

I was floundering terribly.

The Ghost and the Darkness was going and I had to get to South Africa and part of the remains of my brain was trying to deal with changes for that.

I knew generally my problem: I simply was too familiar with *Absolute Power* — I could not free my imagination.

I was simply going nuts — every empty day meant Christmas was that much closer and I had to get it to Eastwood before then or lose him. Here is something most people don't understand: *you never fucking get the actor you want.*

And don't you see, I had a chance for Clint Eastwood in the Clint Eastwood part. *And I wanted that.*

November 15th and good news — maybe Frank Darabond would spitball with me. (Darabond had one of the great directing debuts with *The Shawshank Redemption* and wrote that remarkable script.)

Close but he had other commitments.

November 25th and I haven't started.

And I am drowning.

That night the Knicks beat Houston, (I am not even arguably one of the four all time greatest Knick fans) but even better than the victory was this fact: I took Tony Gilroy to the game.

Tony (*Dolores Claiborne, Extreme Measures*) is someone I have known for thirty years since he was ten, which was when I met and interviewed his father Frank, the Pulitzer-Prize winning playwright. (*The Subject Was Roses.* I was writing a book about Broadway, *The Season.*)

"So what's with *Absolute Power* ?" he asked politely; Tony had read the first draft months and months before.

I told him about what Eastwood wanted. "*Great,*" he said.

At that moment, death by torture would have been letting him off too lightly. "Why?"

"Obvious why — Luther's the best character — when he dies, he takes the movie down with him."

Kind of casually I asked this: "you think you could figure out how to do it?"

He was intent on the game. "Haven't thought about it but it shouldn't be hard."

That night I called Shafer and Tony was hired for a week.

The next morning he came blasting in — "I know where Luther goes after right after the robbery — he goes to see his daughter."

"Can't."

"What do you say that?"

"*They never talk* — Baldacci is very clear on that in the novel — and they don't talk before the murder because they are estranged and they can't after because he's afraid the President will kill her — "

"Forget about the novel   I haven't read the novel — my greatest strength is that I haven't read the novel — *the novel is killing you.*"

"They can't talk and that's it.

"*Think about it, for chrissakes.*"

Shortly thereafter I not only thought about it, I wrote about it. Here's the first **LUTHER–KATE** scene:

CUT TO

A YOUNG WOMAN PARKING HER CAR — a high rocky area above the Patomac. Below, a jogging path is visible, full of runners.

THE YOUNG WOMAN gets out locks her car, starts down a narrow walk toward the joggers.

SHE'S IN THE MID-THIRTIES. Pretty. And there's something familiar about her.

CUT TO

LUTHER, standing by the edge of the jogging path, studying the runners. Now he registers something and smiles.

CUT TO

THE WOMAN IN HER MID-THIRTIES as she comes jogging along. She runs well.

CUT TO

LUTHER. An imperceptible straightening of his clothes.

CUT TO

THE JOGGER. Now we realize who she is: the little girl in the photo on LUTHER's dining room table. All grown up. Now her face registers something: his presence. Her eyes go down to the path, she increases her speed.

CUT TO

LUTHER.

LUTHER

Kate.
                         (she runs on)
Kate.
                (she slows, hesitates, stops.)

CUT TO

KATE, hands on hips, breathing deeply, moving to the edge of the path as he approaches. The river flows behind them. Runners pass by.

Beat

LUTHER
Probably too late for me to take it up.
                (she says nothing — he gestures
                        toward the path)
The jogging.

                              KATE

Ahh.

Beat.

                              LUTHER
Dumb way to start this, I guess.

                              KATE
For a man of your charm.

                              LUTHER
Wanted to talk.

                              KATE
About?

                              LUTHER
Believe it or not, the weather.
                         (she waits)
Nights are starting to get cold.

                              KATE
That happens this time of year.

CUT TO

LUTHER *He speaks quickly now, his voice low.*

                              LUTHER
I was thinking of maybe relocating. Someplace with a kinder cli-
mate.
                    (nothing shows on her face)
I just wanted to check it out with you first...
                         (still nothing)
...you're the only family I've got.
                         (and on that)

CUT TO

KATE. *She speaks quickly now, her voice low.*

KATE

Luther, you don't have me.

The last words in this world he wanted to hear. But you can't tell from looking at him.

KATE

You were never there. Remember? You're talking to the only kid during show and tell who got to talk about visiting day.

LUTHER

I'm talking permanent, you understand.

KATE

We don't see each other anyway — we haven't seen each other since Mom died and that's a year —
        (a step toward him)
— look, you chose your life. You had that fight. You were never around for me. Well, fine. But I have no plans to be around for you.

And now she stops, turns away toward the path — LUTHER can say nothing, watches her —

— then she spins back —

KATE
        (louder now)
— wait a minute — you're lying about something, aren't you?

LUTHER

— no —

KATE

— is that why you're here now? — are you active again?

LUTHER

— no —

KATE moves in close now —

KATE

— I don't believe you —

(big)
— Christ, father what have you done? —

and on her words —

CUT TO

CHRISTY SULLIVAN's *body in the bedroom of the mansion —*

I don't think I can ever explain how freeing that scene was.
These two characters who I had been thinking about for six
months and who had never been allowed to talk to each other
were suddenly ripping at each other. And there's all that emotional father/daughter stuff working under because you know
LUTHER knows if he stays the President will kill him but he's
willing to risk all that just to hear his only child ask him to stay.

I am aware we are not talking about a scene that will change
the course of film history. But God, I was grateful to be able to
write it. I think what I was dealing with was this: I started as a
novelist, was a novelist for a decade before I ever saw a screenplay and in part of my head at least, even though I haven't tried
one in ten years now, I'm still a novelist. And I guess I never
thought I would do that to another novelist, change everything.
God knows it's been done to me — *No Way To Treat A Lady* for
example, was based on this notion: what if there were two
Boston Stranglers and what if one of them got jealous of the
other?

Guess what? In the movie, there's only one strangler. And I
hated that they had done that.

Now here I was doing it.

And thank the Good Lord.

Tony came over for the next days, always bringing ideas with
him. LUTHER should have a safe house. If LUTHER is one of the
great thieves of the world, and he is, there can't be too many like
him and then law enforcement agencies must keep track of
that — which meant SETH AND LUTHER could meet without

SETH doing a great deal of time-wasting detective work.

And most of all Tony solved the ending — because the only person in the story who traditionally has the right to take revenge against **PRESIDENT RICHMOND** is the wronged husband, **WALTER SULLIVAN**. **SULLIVAN** is the reason **RICHMOND** made it to the White House, after all. In the earlier versions as in the novel **SULLIVAN** is murdered by the Secret Service.

Guess what — not this time. He lives and he kills the President — **SULLIVAN AND LUTHER**, two previously dead characters bring down the most powerful man on the face of the earth. And Jack Graham, the hero of the first draft?

Gone.

On the 15th of December I was exhausted. But I was done. I sent the third draft of *Absolute Power* to California.

On the 28th of December, Eastwood said 'yes' to Luther.

And in January I smashed my thumb.

I was closing the refrigerator door and forgot to pull my thumb away in time and I creamed myself and a blood blister formed beneath the nail and it took six months for the blister to work it's way up, to finally disappear.

Every time I looked at it, I was glad — because it reminded me of my most difficult time as a screenwriter. And the fragility of writing careers.

Because I know if I don't take Tony to the Houston game, or if he can't come maybe the movie of *Absolute Power* never happens. Certainly I would no longer have been involved.

I have seen the finished film as I write this and you will decide what you think of it. But I can tell you this: I'm sure glad *I'm* involved.

There, now you know everything.

ABSOLUTE POWER

FADE IN ON

THE SADDEST EYES YOU EVER SAW

We are looking at an El Greco drawing. It is a study for one of his paintings.

PULL BACK TO REVEAL.

We are in a large museum — a bunch of art students are doing sketches of the eyes, the elongated hands, the slender hands El Greco drew so brilliantly.

Most of the students are around 20. A couple of suburban housewives are there too.

And one older man.

This is LUTHER WHITNEY. *Mid 60s, very fit, neatly dressed. At quick glance, he seems as if he might be a successful company executive.*

As we watch him draw we can tell he is capable of great concentration. And patient. With eyes that miss nothing: he has pilot's eyes.

We'll find out more about him as time goes on, but this is all you really have to know: LUTHER WHITNEY *is the hero of this piece. As we watch him draw —*

CREDITS START TO ROLL.

CUT TO

LUTHER'S SKETCHBOOK. He is finishing his work on the eyes, and he's caught the sadness: it's good stuff.

CUT TO

LUTHER. It's not good enough for him. He looks at his work a moment, shakes his head.

> **GIRL STUDENT**
> Don't give up.

> **LUTHER**
> I never do.

> **GIRL STUDENT**
> May I?

> *(she's indicated his sketchbook. He*
> *nods. She starts thumbing through)*

CUT TO

THE SKETCHBOOK AS THE PAGES TURN.

Detail work. Eyes and hands. The eyes are good. The hands are better. Very skillful.

THE GIRL *hands it back. Impressed.*

> ### GIRL STUDENT
> You work with your hands, don't you?

CUT TO

LUTHER. CLOSE UP. *An enigmatic smile. Now, from that —*

CUT TO

A NICE WORKING CLASS PART OF TOWN.

Nothing fancy here but there's a pleasant feel. The streets are clean, the houses neat and well tended.

LUTHER, *carrying his sketchbook, walks along. It's afternoon now. Up ahead is a local bar:* RED'S.

CUT TO

INSIDE THE BAR AS LUTHER *walks in. Nothing fancy here. Strictly working class. And relatively empty. An overweight bald man* LUTHER's *age works behind the bar. This is* RED. *They are good enough friends not to ask each other questions.*

> ### LUTHER
> *(they nod to each other)*
> Redhead.

> ### RED
> Luther.
> *(*LUTHER *hands him a videotape)*
> Your life would be a whole lot simpler if you could learn to operate a VCR.

LUTHER

My only failing.

(as he turns).

CUT TO

A STREET OF SMALL ROW HOUSES.

Clean, well tended.

LUTHER walks toward one. Later in the afternoon. He carries half a dozen small shopping bags, from the market, the hardware store, the drug store, the cleaners.

CUT TO

A TERRA COTTA PLANTER to the right of the front door. Luther shifts his packages, tilts the planter slightly, bends down, pulls out a key, inserts it in the front door.

CUT TO

THE KITCHEN INSIDE as he enters. Neat, tidy. A Cuisinart, a cheese slicer, lots of other nice equipment. As he begins putting food away —

CUT TO

THE DINING AREA. Evening now. Table set for one. A single candle. Beside the candle is LUTHER's sketch pad. Now LUTHER himself moves into view, carrying a tray. He puts it down.

A gorgeous omelet is on a fine china plate, parsley sprinkled neatly on top. An elegant green salad is on another plate, covered with thinly sliced parmesan cheese. An expensive water pitcher, a lovely glass. Clearly, a great deal of thought has gone into dinner.

LUTHER lights the single candle. We are now aware of a photograph nearby. The picture is old. A pretty little girl stands in the center, smiling. Her mother stands alongside, smiling too. A MAN is with them, looking at them happily. It's LUTHER. When he was young.

LUTHER studies the photo a moment. Then he turns, looks out the window.

A SLIVER OF MOON IS VISIBLE.

Lovely. Peaceful.

Now LUTHER *opens the sketch pad, quickly flips past the hands and eyes and faces —*

— we are looking at something totally different: <u>a mansion</u>.

HOLD ON LUTHER'S DRAWING OF THE MANSION.

CREDITS COME TO AN END.

KEEP HOLDING.

PULL BACK TO REVEAL

THE MANSION ITSELF. IN THE MOONLIGHT —

— it looks exactly like his drawing.

But no drawing could convey the size of the place — we are looking at ten thousand square feet. Wealth and power.

We're in rolling hill country.

The mansion is dark.

Totally deserted.

Silence.

Now a sound — tires on gravel.

A car comes rolling into view.

The motor of the car has been turned off.

The lights of the car have been turned off.

The car slides to a stop.

Again, silence . . .

HOLD ON THE MANSION, *a couple of hundred yards away. There is a small, rectangular cornfield between the car and the estate. Now —*

CUT TO

INSIDE THE CAR. A MAN holds binoculars, studying the place. He wears dark clothes, tennis shoes. He puts down the binoculars, begins to smear his face with black camouflage cream —

— it's LUTHER, and he's been a professional thief his entire life. He's a three time loser, but his last sentence was so long ago and his skills are now so vast, so refined, that it is unlikely he will ever get caught again.

CUT TO

THE CORNFIELD AS LUTHER glides through it. He wears a backpack.

The night is cool.

He comes to the edge of the cornfield, stops. All that separates him from the mansion now is a stretch of gorgeous lawn. Except for LUTHER, it isn't gorgeous it's no man's land.

One final check of his surroundings —

— then he sets off, in graceful motion, long strides eating up the ground. He makes no sound at all.

CUT TO

THE FRONT DOOR. Thick wood with reinforced steel.

LUTHER stops by the door, takes off his backpack, opens it.

He puts on plastic gloves that have a special layer of padding at the fingertips and palms.

Now he takes a key, inserts it in the front door, turns it, and the instant he pushes the door open —

ZOOM TO

THE INFRARED SECURITY DETECTOR ACROSS THE FOYER — it immediately starts to beep and you can see the seconds being counted down: FORTY, THIRTY-NINE, THIRTY —

CUT TO

LUTHER — in his hands now is an automatic screwdriver, no more than six inches long —

— he sets to work on the security panel that is inside in the foyer next to the front door.

The screwdriver undoes the first screw, the second —

CUT TO

THE SECURITY DETECTOR — *THIRTY-ONE, THIRTY, TWENTY-NINE*

CUT TO

THE SCREWDRIVER.

Now the third and fourth screws are in LUTHER's *hands and he lifts the security panel away.*

The beeping sound is constant —

— and getting louder.

CUT TO

A TINY DEVICE, *no bigger than a pocket calculator. It has two wires protruding from it. It is, we are about to find out, a tiny computer.* LUTHER *holds it like a baby.*

CUT TO

THE SECURITY DETECTOR — *EIGHTEEN, SEVENTEEN —*

CUT TO

LUTHER, *probing with the wires into the heart of the security panel.*

The beeping is louder still.

CUT TO

THE SECURITY PANEL.

LUTHER *is attempting delicate work and it's dark so it isn't easy but he continues to probe with the wires and —*

CUT TO

THE SECURITY DETECTOR. *ELEVEN, TEN —*

CUT TO

LUTHER, *and he's got it attached!*

Now the face of the tiny computer is alive with numbers — they fly by much too fast for us to make them out clearly.

CUT TO

THE SECURITY DETECTOR. FOUR, THREE, TWO —

CUT TO

THE FACE OF THE TINY COMPUTER *as five numbers lock* —7 — 13 — 19 — 8 — 11 —

THE BEEPING SOUND DIES.

CUT TO

LUTHER. *A glance across the foyer — the lights of the security detector go from red to a warm looking green.*

Safe.

He allows himself to exhale.

Then he's busy again, unhooking the computer. His fingers, as always, work quickly, precisely.

CUT TO

THE FOYER AS LUTHER, *once again carrying his backpack, moves across it. Behind him, the front door is again shut, the security panel back on, screws all in place.*

It's as if he hadn't been there at all . . .

CUT TO

THE STAIRS *as he walks quickly up — and here we get a sense of the vast size of the place   it feels bigger inside than it looked in the moonlight.*

CUT TO

A VAN GOGH *at the head of the stairs.* LUTHER *moves past it, then stops, goes back, studies the painting. It's a late one, when the madness had him and things were sliding away. Very sad.*

LUTHER *looks at it admiringly for another moment —*

— then surprisingly he raises his hands and for just an instant traces the lines of the painting in the air, as if trying to figure out how the magic was done, as if getting ready for his next museum session —

— then almost grudgingly, he moves on, up toward the third floor.

CUT TO

THE THIRD FLOOR LANDING. *Here's a* HOPPER. *One of the great ones, filled with an overpowering sense of being alone —*

— LUTHER *stares at it almost in awe, whispers "wow," moves on.*

CUT TO

LUTHER, *walking down the third floor corridor.*

CUT TO

THE CORRIDOR WALLS. *No paintings here — instead we see a series of framed photographs. The first is of a baby girl, the next one of the same child at three.*

We watch the child grow up in these photos. At ten she is already pretty. At fifteen a stunner. Not a classic beauty by any means, she is turning into, if you will, a latter day Ann-Margret. The kind of girl you ached for in high school. The perfect cheerleader.

These are pictures, we will come to know, of CHRISTY SULLIVAN. *A high school graduation shot at eighteen, a shot in front of a Burger King at twenty.*

CUT TO

A WEDDING PHOTOGRAPH IN CLOSE UP. CHRISTY, *looking just fabulous, is 24 and smiling happily. We can only see her face and the wedding veil here. Now —*

PULL BACK TO REVEAL

A GLORIOUS AND EXPENSIVE WHITE WEDDING DRESS. CHRISTY *holds a bouquet of flowers. Breathtaking.*

KEEP PULLING BACK

And now we can see the groom. WALTER SULLIVAN. WALTER is smiling too, one arm proudly around his lovely bride.

WALTER, it might be noted, is eighty years old.

CUT TO

LUTHER, staring at the photo, shaking his head. Now he moves on and at last we

CUT TO

THE MASTER BEDROOM. LUTHER opens the door. It squeaks. He goes inside, closes the door firmly. Next, he puts his backpack down, takes out a low power non-glare work light, sets it up. Now he looks around. A huge room, a gigantic canopied bed. A nightstand alongside, which contains a small silver clock, three Danielle Steel novels piled neatly one atop the other, several more photos of the happy couple —

— and an antique silver plated letter opener with a thick leather handle.

CUT TO

LUTHER. He studies himself in front of a very large full length mirror across from the canopied bed.

Now we realize something — he isn't studying himself, he's studying the mirror.

He turns, goes to the sitting area where there are chairs and a sofa and a large TV and VCR.

CUT TO

THREE REMOTES ON A SIDE TABLE. LUTHER carefully picks up the middle one, crosses the room with it, points it at the large mirror, clicks once —

— and the mirror swings silently open.

A room is revealed.

All we can see of it so far is this: there is an armchair in the middle facing where the mirror had been.

LUTHER *turns back toward the sitting area, the remote held in his hand.*

CUT TO

THE SIDE TABLE. LUTHER *puts the remote down — very carefully. In the exact position it had been. Now he takes a moment, blows on his hands, rubs them together.*

CUT TO

LUTHER. *He takes a collapsible duffel bag out of his backpack, moves with the work light into the revealed room —*

CUT TO

THE ROOM — IT'S A VAULT! AND IT'S FULL! *There's cash, naturally, piles of the stuff. Plus all kinds of other valuables we'll get around to.*

LUTHER's *a little stunned — it's more than he hoped for.*

He glances at the armchair — there is a remote on it that is identical to the one he replaced at the side table.

Now he opens his duffel all the way and sets to work.

First the cash goes in — all neatly bundled. Large denominations. Lots of bundles. Next are a series of slender boxes —

CUT TO

THE FIRST BOX AS LUTHER *opens it.*

Jewelry.

Into the duffel it goes.

CUT TO

LUTHER, *emptying more jewelry boxes into the duffel. And still more. As he continues to do this —*

CUT TO

THE BEDROOM. *All is quiet. High on a wall, the security light beams a friendly green.*

Now, from somewhere, a distant sound.

Laughter? Was it laughter?

Doesn't matter, it's gone.

CUT TO

LUTHER IN THE VAULT. *He has moved deeper into it — he's finished with the jewelry. Now he's examining piles of bonds.*

Into the duffel they go.

He takes a breath, glances around.

Perfect.

CUT TO

COINS. *Antique ones. They disappear into the duffel.*

CUT TO

STAMP BOOKS. *Gone into the swelling duffel.*

CUT TO

LUTHER *as he hears now the distant laughter.*

Not so perfect.

He moves quickly out of the VAULT, *takes a step toward the door—the giggling is getting louder, closer. Two people. A* MAN AND A WOMAN.

LUTHER *stops, mutters "shit!" — glances around —*

CUT TO

THE ROOM. *No place to hide.*

CUT TO

LUTHER, *grabbing his backpack, moving into the* VAULT, *turning off his work-light, carefully pulling the door shut —*

— the door clicks —

— *LUTHER is alone in the darkness.*

A burst of laughter now. Growing nearer still.

LUTHER moves into the back of the VAULT, crouches down, doing his best to hide behind the armchair.

Trapped, LUTHER waits in silence, trying not to breathe . . .

Now he can hear a squeak — the bedroom door has opened.

HOLD.

CUT TO

THE BEDROOM. DARK — except for a slant of light from the hall outside the open bedroom door.

TWO PEOPLE are briefly visible as they enter, a man and a woman. The clink of glass. Stifled laughter.

THE WOMAN closes the bedroom door.

Darkness again.

And now the laughing sound increases. Giggling really.

CUT TO

LUTHER in the pitch black VAULT. The giggling is muted but it is there. He is starting to perspire.

CUT TO

THE BEDROOM. THE WOMAN flicks on the lights and as she does —

ZOOM TO

LUTHER AS THE BURST OF LIGHT HITS HIM LIKE A FIST — AND IT'S OVER, IT'S DONE, HE'S BEEN CAUGHT.

LUTHER blinks, confused, looks around —

— because it isn't over, he hasn't been caught.

The door to the vault is suddenly <u>gone</u>. LUTHER is staring STRAIGHT into the goddam bedroom.

Because the door is a one way mirror. Now it's as if he was watching the bedroom on a giant TV screen.

Just a few feet away, just outside the door.

Where things are clearly starting to heat up.

LUTHER moves to the armchair, sits. There is nothing to do now but wait. He settles in as we

CUT TO

THE BEDROOM. They are staring at each other.

We have seen the woman already — she's CHRISTY SULLIVAN. But the pictures in the corridor did not do her justice.

This is a fabulous looking twenty-five year old woman. Long, golden hair, a round face that sets off her deep blue eyes, a tanned, curving body. A bare shouldered black dress. An expensive necklace.

One more thing: she is staggering drunk.

THE MAN IS ALAN RICHMOND, wealthy, successful, handsome and fit. Mid-forties. He wears an elegantly cut suit.

Two additional points: (1) RICHMOND is clearly not the husband in the wedding photo. (2) He is drunker than she is.

RICHMOND carries a vodka bottle and two tumblers. He fills them, gives one to her.

They touch glasses.

Down the hatch.

Tight laughter.

He looks at her.

She looks at him. There's a lot of sexual tension in the air.

But now he begins looking around, checking things out. She spots this.

CHRISTY
(drunk)
It's okay — I told him I was sick — anyway, he's gone — relax...

He nods then, more at ease. And he blows her a kiss.

She catches it —

— and now she starts to parade for him. Her body moving very slowly.

He pours himself another shot, chugs it, watches. Now —

CUT TO

LUTHER *suddenly terrified and we find out why as we*

CUT TO

CHRISTY, *fumbling with her necklace, looks across the room —*

CUT TO

What she's looking at: the side table with the remote that opens the VAULT.

CUT TO

LUTHER, *frozen, as* CHRISTY *starts toward the table.*

CUT TO

THE TABLE *and the remote waiting there.*

CUT TO

LUTHER, *mouth dry...*

CUT TO

RICHMOND, *reaching out for her then as she passes him; he takes her by the hand —*

— and now they are dancing, their bodies pressed together. They move slowly. She hums. He tries to get fancy, spin her with one arm —

— no good. They're too drunk for it, start to lose balance, separate.

They giggle. Smile at each other. Now CHRISTY *manages to unhook her necklace, and as she starts to drop it to the floor —*

CUT TO

LUTHER. *A genuine sigh of relief —*

—- which suddenly <u>dies</u> —

CUT TO

CHRISTY, *as she spins toward the table again, still with the necklace in her hand.*

CUT TO

LUTHER, *and there's nothing he can do now but watch as we*

CUT TO

RICHMOND, *watching too, emptying the vodka bottle into his tumbler, chugging it down and now*

CUT TO

THE TABLE *as* CHRISTY *reaches out, grabs a remote, turns and*

CUT TO

LUTHER *dead in the water —*

— because she's pointing the goddam thing at him —

—<u> and as she clicks it</u>

CUT TO

LUTHER, *and for a moment, he's like a goddam deer caught in the headlights —*

— but now here comes another sigh of relief and we find out why as we

CUT TO

THE BEDROOM *as suddenly there's romantic music playing —she's turned the stereo on.* CHRISTY *starts humming, replaces the clicker, drops the necklace to the floor.*

Then they are into each other's arms. Their bodies press. Their bodies sway. He moves a hand to her breasts —

— CHRISTY breaks loose, shakes a finger at him, as if to say, "naughty naughty" —

— then with.one hand, she pulls a zipper down. The dress falls off her body. Her breasts spring free. She is wearing only her panties now and high heels. And a smile.

She is stunning looking and she knows it and men have always gone nuts over her and she knows that too. And RICHMOND can't resist her either, goes to her, bends her back, caresses her neck, begins sucking her nipples. CHRISTY moans.

CUT TO

LUTHER, in the chair, embarrassed, averting his eyes.

But the moaning from the other room grows louder, more insistent.

CUT TO

CHRISTY, pulling away for a moment, starting to work at RICHMOND's tie, shakes him out of his suit jacket, reaches for his belt, loosens it. She is working at his shirt buttons now and their breathing is audible and in a moment he is down to his boxer shorts and then her panties are off, her shoes kicked away and they are near the vault mirror now and

CUT TO

THE VAULT MIRROR as they approach it, stare at themselves.

CUT TO

LUTHER, moving farther back in his chair as their faces are just a couple of feet away —

CUT TO

CHRISTY, close up, as his hands move across her wondrous body and she is hot and drifting into drunken fantasy and her eyes close and

CUT TO

RICHMOND, CLOSE UP, and his eyes are open —

— and the look on his drunken face is <u>scary</u>.

CUT TO

LUTHER, *transfixed by that look, transfixed and worried and*

CUT TO

CHRISTY AND RICHMOND IN CLOSE UP, *looking at each other now, and she is smiling happily and looking at him and he is smiling happily and looking at her, and whatever was on his face just before has gone.*

CUT TO

LUTHER, *watching as they turn for the gigantic canopied bed.*

CUT TO

THE BED *as they stop alongside it and kiss — it's their first. And her arms go around his neck and she holds him like that, her eyes shut tight —*

CUT TO

LUTHER *— watching because* RICHMOND's *eyes are not shut, they are wide open and they stare at the mirror and the awful look from before is back only worse and then without warning he grips her buttocks roughly —*

and slaps her hand on the ass, over and over and

CUT TO

CHRISTY, *shocked, surprised, pulling away and*

CUT TO

RICHMOND, *smiling at her sweetly.*

CUT TO

CHRISTY. *Shaking her head.*

CUT TO

RICHMOND. *He continues to smile, makes a courtly gesture, kissing her finger-tips in apology.*

CUT TO

CHRISTY. She smiles in acknowledgment and they move onto the bed. She pushes him down.

And straddles him.

CUT TO

RICHMOND, from her point of view — a wonderfully handsome man.

CUT TO

CHRISTY, from his point of view. A glorious, vibrant young woman. She smiles, touches her lips to a finger, reaches out, touches the finger to his mouth.

It's a sweet moment.

They smile.

Then he reaches up, and without a word, grabs her breasts and squeezes and twists them brutally and CHRISTY is shocked and she tries to make him stop but he won't and she cries out in pain but he still won't stop so she slaps him in the face. He slaps her back, viciously, right in the mouth and now there is blood mixing with her lipstick and she rolls off the bed onto the floor.

CUT TO

THE FLOOR AS CHRISTY sits there stunned.

> **CHRISTY**
> *(slurred)*

You fucking bastard.

> *(and on that —)*

CUT TO

RICHMOND, standing now, he reaches down to help her up. CHRISTY hesitates, finally takes his hand and as soon as she is on her feet —

CUT TO

CHRISTY, kicking him all she has in the stomach and

CUT TO

LUTHER, *silently applauding and*

CUT TO

RICHMOND, *the air momentarily out of him, falling drunkenly to the floor, stunned for just a moment and clearly in pain, but he is a big man and he is strong and he grabs her ankle, yanks, and then both are laboring on the floor and*

CUT TO

CHRISTY, *kicking him, again and again —*

— but he will not release her ankle. Each kick only inflames his drunken rage.

RICHMOND
(very slurred —)
You cunt, you little whore —

And now they both try and stand.

Neither one does it gracefully, neither one does it quickly, but RICHMOND gets there first and as soon as he is on his feet he begins to strangle her.

CUT TO

CHRISTY, *gasping, terrified, she claws at his arms, her fingers scratching deeply — but he will not let go.*

She twists and jerks her body —

— no good — he continues to tighten his grip on her throat —

— and spreads his legs for better balance.

CUT TO

THE BED TABLE AS CHRISTY, *beyond desperation reaches around for something, anything — her fingers finally close on the letter opener and in one wild stroke, she slashes his left arm.*

Now he lets go.

And stares, stunned, at his bleeding arm.

Then he crunches her flush in the mouth, a brutal blow and blood pours from

her nose and mouth and if she weren't so scared, maybe it would have stopped her, but it doesn't — because somehow she manages to maintain balance —

— and knees him all she has in the nuts.

It's over — RICHMOND falls to the floor, helpless. He lies on his back, holding his crotch.

CUT TO

But it isn't over. CHRISTY, blood pouring down her face stands over him, the letter opener still tight in her hand.

And in her eyes you can see it, the homicidal rage —

— and she drops to her knees beside him —

— and RICHMOND can only lie there, watching her —

— and she gets a better grip on the letter opener —

— and RICHMOND still only lies there, watching her—

— and she raises the letter opener slowly very high above her head, the point aimed at his heart

— and RICHMOND screams one time —

— and as CHRISTY starts to kill him, TWO WELL DRESSED MEN in business suits burst through the bedroom doorway, guns in their hands, and they blow her brains out before the opener reaches RICHMOND's heart.

CUT TO

LUTHER, IN SLOW MOTION and this is what he does —

— he reels back in the chair, eyes wide, jaw slack, mouth open —

— this is a man who has seen everything but nothing has prepared him for this —

— his arms flop over the arms of the chair, his body loses strength, he tries to look away, can't —

— and this is what he sees —

CUT TO

CHRISTY, fighting for another instant of life —

— no chance —

— the two bullets have shattered her brain, her eyes roll up into her head, the letter opener drops to the rug, she collapses like a rag doll —

— and blood is everywhere.

CUT TO

LUTHER. Back in regular motion now. Pale, barely able to breathe.

CUT TO

THE TWO WELL DRESSED MEN IN BUSINESS SUITS.

BILL BURTON is the more formidable. Mid-40's, he looks like a retired tight end. No body fat. Intimidating. But right now he is shaking and he can't stop it.

He puts his gun away, goes to RICHMOND.

TIM COLLIN is closing in on 30. Handsome. In wonderful shape. BURTON is more physical, COLLIN more lethal.

He puts his gun away, goes to CHRISTY.

RICHMOND is trying to sit. He is as drunk as before but now he is also close to shock. He reaches over, manages to pick up the bloody letter opener.

> **RICHMOND**
> Kill her?
>> *(COLLIN, by the body, nods)*

> **BURTON**
> No choice in the matter.
>> *(his words are efficient but clearly,*
>> *he has been rocked)*

CUT TO

RICHMOND, *staring stupidly at the letter opener. He drops it back to the floor, tries to stand, can't.*

BURTON *helps him back to the bed.*

Which is when he passes out cold.

BURTON AND COLLIN *look at each other now.*

> ### BURTON
> Jesus, Tim, what did we do?

> ### COLLIN
> *(echoing BURTON)*
> No choice in the matter.

CUT TO

LUTHER, *staring at it all. The shock is still there but so is something new: <u>anger</u>. And on that —*

CUT TO

GLORIA RUSSELL *moving through the bedroom door. RUSSELL's 40, well dressed, attractive and <u>very smart</u>. Now she sees what's happened, stops dead.*

Now she moves forward, looks at BURTON AND COLLIN. It's very clear from the outset: <u>these three are not friendly</u>.

> ### RUSSELL
> *(to BURTON and COLLIN)*
> Do you realize what a shitstorm we're in?
> *(beat)*
> Go on — tell me.

> ### COLLIN
> Nothing to tell. He screamed.

> ### RUSSELL
> And you heard no sounds of violence 'til then?

> ### BURTON
> *(beat)*
> Nothing we haven't heard before.

CUT TO

RICHMOND, on the bed, out. RUSSELL studies his face as BURTON moves toward the telephone.

> **BURTON**
> Maybe I should call the police now.

CUT TO

RUSSELL IN CLOSE UP.

> **RUSSELL**
> *(soft)*
> Bill? Why don't you think about that?
> *(beat — starting to move toward him)*
> Take a second and just think about that.
> *(closing in on BURTON, furious)*
> Think...real...fucking...hard.

CUT TO

BURTON. He is strong enough to snap her neck with one hand.

> **BURTON**
> *(backing away)*
> Probably not a good idea.

> **RUSSELL**
> *(taking charge)*
> Okay — here's what happened tonight — poor Christy came home alone and interrupted a burglary. That sound logical?

CUT TO

LUTHER in the closet. He nods.

CUT TO

BURTON AND COLLIN. They nod too.

> **RUSSELL**
> We're going to have to sanitize this place.

> *(shaking RICHMOND)*

Alan, did you have sex with her?

CUT TO

RICHMOND, eyes barely open.

RICHMOND
...don'...'member...

RUSSELL
Bill, you're going to have to examine her.

BURTON
I'm no gynecologist.

RUSSELL
> *(she takes nothing from nobody)*

I just made you one.
> *(end of discussion. Now —)*

CUT TO

A CLOCK ON THE SIDETABLE BESIDE THE THREE CLICKERS.

There is the sound of a vacuum — it's later now.

CUT TO

THE MASTER BEDROOM. The place is incredibly changed. CHRISTY is lying as before — except now she is fully dressed. The bed has been made with clean sheets. There is a large black plastic garbage bag that COLLIN shoves the sheets in; BURTON is vacuuming the rug.

RICHMOND is visible, still in terrible shape, finishing putting his clothes on in the open master bathroom.

Everyone wears gloves.

Everything that is incriminating is gone —

— except the letter opener which has been put in a clear plastic bag. COLLIN reaches for it, starts to dump it in along with the sheets and the jewelry.

> RUSSELL

I'll take that.

> COLLIN
> (surprised)

It's got their prints on it.

> RUSSELL
> (she holds out her hand)

Thanks for sharing.
> (COLLIN glances at BURTON,
> shrugs, hands it over. RUSSELL puts
> it in her handbag, puts the
> handbag on the bed table when
> suddenly —)

CUT TO

RICHMOND, careening into the room, wide-eyed, crying out —

> RICHMOND

Gloria — I killed her —

CUT TO

RUSSELL, turning, shocked as RICHMOND bears down —

— she holds out her arms for him but he is staggering and he collides hard with her, spins against the wall, uses the bed table to try and steady himself and

CUT TO

LUTHER, stunned, staring and now

CUT TO

WHAT HE'S STARING AT: the letter opener has spilled from her open purse and fallen behind the bed out of sight.

CUT TO

RUSSELL, calm, going to RICHMOND, starting to lead him from the room —

> RUSSELL

It's all going to be fine, Alan.

> **RICHMOND**
> ... but she's dead ...

> **RUSSELL**
> ... I'll take care of everything, just like I always do.
> *(to* BURTON *and* COLLIN*)*
> Gentlemen?
> *(she gestures to leave)*

BURTON AND COLLIN *finish up —* COLLIN *grabs the large plastic bag.* BURTON *glances around one final time and backs toward the door, vacuuming carefully. Then —*

CUT TO

COLLIN AS HE STOPS DEAD. *He stares across at the bed table.*

CUT TO

LUTHER, *holding his breath.*

CUT TO

BURTON AND COLLIN.

> **COLLIN**
> Shit.

> **BURTON**
> What?

In reply, COLLIN *dashes back toward the bed table, grabs* RUSSELL's *purse, snaps it shut, tucks it under one arm and leaves.*

BURTON *flicks the light out, closes the door.*

The room is lit by moonlight now. CHRISTY *looks beautiful and still.* HOLD FOR A MOMENT. THEN—

CUT TO

THE FRONT DOOR OF THE MANSION.

It's open and RUSSELL *leads a staggering* RICHMOND *outside. A very long black limousine is parked in the driveway.*

BURTON is behind them, turning off all the lights. COLLIN is last, with RUSSELL's purse, the garbage bag. As he follows them outside, he closes the front door firmly —it makes a loud, solid sound.

CUT TO

LUTHER IN THE VAULT. The sound is barely audible. He has been looking at his watch —

CUT TO

THE WATCH FACE, illuminated in the darkness. The second hand is fifteen seconds away from the top.

CUT TO

LUTHER. He takes a breath, waits in silence.

CUT TO

THE WATCH FACE. The sound is loud, like <u>60 Minutes</u>.

CUT TO

BURTON AND RUSSELL moving with RICHMOND toward the car. BURTON takes the man in his arms leaving RUSSELL free to open the back door.

COLLIN dumps the plastic bag into the trunk, shuts it, moves quickly so that he can get a decent view of the road.

CUT TO

THE ROAD IN FRONT OF THE HOUSE. Empty. COLLIN hurries to the limo where BURTON is struggling to get RICHMOND comfortably stretched out on the back seat.

CUT TO

THE WATCH FACE. The second hand hits the top and LUTHER moves into action —

— he points the clicker at the door —

— the door starts to swing open —

— LUTHER, backpack in hand, strides quickly into the bedroom, turns, points the clicker again and as the door starts to swing shut —

CUT TO

LUTHER, carefully tossing the clicker back inside and

CUT TO

THE ARMCHAIR as the clicker lands — dead solid perfect —

CUT TO

LUTHER, in the bedroom, moving to the nightstand, carrying his backpack —

— he slows as he circles the body of CHRISTY SULLIVAN, looks sadly down at her, continues on as we

CUT TO

THE BED TABLE. LUTHER, tense, kneels, probes behind it, reaches farther and then —

CUT TO

THE LETTER OPENER! In the plastic bag. LUTHER grabs it.

CUT TO

LUTHER rises, opener in hand, and goes to the far window that looks out on the rear of the house.

Now he puts the letter opener carefully inside his backpack, takes out a coil of knotted rope.

Then he moves across the bedroom to a window that has a view of the front of the house. He looks out, grimaces.

CUT TO

THE FRONT OF THE HOUSE. The limousine is still there. BURTON is visible helping RUSSELL in. COLLIN hands over her purse, closes the door. He and BURTON move to the front doors.

CUT TO

LUTHER, going to the rear window. He opens the window slowly and silently. He ties one end of the rope around the leg of a heavy wooden chest of drawers —

— now he carefully plays the knotted rope out the window.

CUT TO

INSIDE THE LIMOUSINE AS BURTON AND COLLIN are getting settled in the front. RICHMOND lies in a stupor stretched along the rear seat and in the seat opposite, RUSSELL —

— a moment of relief. They breathe deep. And as RUSSELL starts to open her purse —

CUT TO

THE KNOTTED ROPE as it snakes down the brick mansion — it reaches the ground and

CUT TO

LUTHER, putting his backpack on securely.

CUT TO

THE WINDOW — LUTHER glances out and down and

CUT TO

THE GROUND — forty feet below. And it's dark.

CUT TO

LUTHER — he doesn't much like this — but taking hold of the rope, he puts one leg out the window — only the damn backpack makes it complicated and he's caught for a moment, clumsily trapped with one leg in, one leg out and the backpack wedged against the corner of the window —

— and at that moment, there is a <u>scream</u> and we

ZOOM TO

GLORIA RUSSELL in the car, as every nightmare she has ever had comes true — the fucking letter opener isn't in her purse and as she screams again —

CUT TO

LUTHER, *cursing to himself, forcing his way out the window and it isn't easy but he makes it —*

— and then the rope slips in his hands and for one precarious moment he is in serious trouble and

CUT TO

THE LIMO DOORS BUSTING OPEN AS BURTON AND COLLIN *come barreling out and*

CUT TO

LUTHER, *getting his grip on the nylon rope again, starting to go down — but it's difficult going for him and*

CUT TO

BURTON AND COLLIN *tearing into the house,* COLLIN *in the lead and*

CUT TO

LUTHER IN THE NIGHT, *thirty feet up, and he can hear commotion inside the house and he tries to go faster —*

— but it's not easy; the man is, after all, in his 60's and he's dangerously high and his visibility is rotten so he's doing the best he can, but he isn't exactly flying and

CUT TO

RUSSELL, *standing by the limo, staring in at the house and from the look on her face you know she thinks her life might be over and*

CUT TO

BURTON AND COLLIN, *racing up the second floor staircase toward the top and*

CUT TO

LUTHER, *half-way down and*

CUT TO

BURTON AND COLLIN, tearing along the third floor corridor.

CUT TO

LUTHER, ten feet off the ground now.

CUT TO

THE BEDROOM DOOR, flying open.

CUT TO

LUTHER, six feet to go, three, and he lets go, drops the rest of the way, hits the ground running and

CUT TO

BURTON, racing toward the window, COLLIN goes to the night table and

CUT TO

LUTHER, at the end of the house, turning a corner and

CUT TO

BURTON, staring out the window and LUTHER is <u>gone</u>.

BURTON

Shit!

CUT TO

COLLIN, looking around the night table and the letter opener is <u>gone</u>.

COLLIN

Shit!

And without another word, they bolt out the door.

CUT TO

LUTHER, crashing through the cornfield. He is in wonderful shape —

— for a man his age.

And he gives it all he has but is it going to be enough?

CUT TO

THE LIMOUSINE AS COLLIN *yanks something out of the glove compartment, and then he is racing off into the night after* BURTON *who is a few steps ahead and*

CUT TO

RUSSELL *staring after them — in the back seat,* RICHMOND *is in a half slumber.*

CUT TO

LUTHER, *bursting out of the cornfield —*

— up ahead is the most dangerous place for him —

— one hundred yards of open field. He runs on.

CUT TO

BURTON AND COLLIN, *as* COLLIN *catches up to the other man, tosses what he took from the glove compartment.*

Thermal goggles.

They put them on on the fly and

CUT TO

THE WORLD AHEAD OF THEM AS THEY SEE IT: *their field of vision now resembles a rough computer game. Thermal images register in red, everything else is dark green.*

CUT TO

LUTHER. *Beginning to tire now — and he's only halfway through the open field and*

CUT TO

BURTON AND COLLIN, *behind him, can't see him yet, but they are moving faster —*

— and BURTON *could probably destroy anyone in a fight —*

— but COLLIN *can fly.*

And he begins to leave BURTON *behind.*

CUT TO

LUTHER, *and twenty yards ahead of him are some woods and that spurs him on, he pumps his arms, his body straining and his breath coming in gasps and*

CUT TO

COLLIN, *graceful and young and in fabulous shape and just ahead is the open field and as he starts into it —*

CUT TO

WHAT COLLIN SEES: *a thermal figure; a man running out of the open field and then disappearing into the woods.*

CUT TO

THE OPEN FIELD *and the sight of the figure is enough to kick* COLLIN *into overdrive and he has never run this fast as he crosses the open area and*

CUT TO

LUTHER, *running through the woods — he can hear them now, and he knows they're closing on him and he glances back —*

— and smashes into a fucking tree! . . . hard . . . and it rocks him, drops him to his knees —

CUT TO

COLLIN *and he could be jet propelled and*

CUT TO

LUTHER, *forcing himself back to his feet and running again, giving it everything he has left and he's dodging through the trees now and*

CUT TO

BURTON, *behind* COLLIN, *but he draws his gun anyway and*

CUT TO

COLLIN in the woods, and his gun's drawn too and

CUT TO

LUTHER, out of the woods and now his car is visible and

CUT TO

COLLIN, in the woods but they're coming to an end and

CUT TO

WHAT HE SEES: the figure up ahead is approaching a car and

CUT TO

LUTHER, throwing the car door open, ripping off his backpack, tossing it inside, jumping in behind the wheel and

CUT TO

BURTON. Pulling up, gasping terribly. He sinks to one knee.

CUT TO

COLLIN, out of the woods! —

— still amazingly without the least sign of tiring —

— and now there is a sound: a car motor starting.

CUT TO

LUTHER in his car, wheels spinning and

CUT TO

COLLIN has his pistol ready but it's impossible to hit anything when you're running like this and

CUT TO

LUTHER, in the car, gunning away and

CUT TO

COLLIN. Slowing.

CUT TO

THE CAR. *A swirl of dust.*

The dust clears.

The car rounds a corner, is gone.

CUT TO

COLLIN. *He stands there, rips off his thermal goggles —*

— and surprisingly, he <u>smiles</u>.

CUT TO

BURTON, *getting to his feet, his breath still not steady. He takes his goggles off too as* COLLIN *approaches.*

> **COLLIN**
> *(still the smile)*

I got his license number.
> *(now on that —)*

CUT TO

RUSSELL — *back in the master bedroom, with* BURTON *and* COLLIN *who are moving around constantly, checking the place out. Things are just amazingly tense.*

> **RUSSELL**
> *(close to losing it)*

Gee, guys, maybe it was the boogeyman — don't forget to check under the bed —
> *(exploding)*
— you may have <u>buried</u> us! —

> **COLLIN**

— relax, I got his license number, remember? —

> **RUSSELL**
> *(whirling on him)*

— you think he's going to just sit around waiting for us? — asshole —

COLLIN
— take it easy, Miss Russell —

BURTON
(trying for calm)
— <u>everybody shut up, all right?</u>

He is staring at his reflection in the big mirror. He crosses to it, goes to his knees, studies the rug.

CUT TO

THE RUG — *indentations in the expensive carpet.*

BURTON
Oh boy...

CUT TO

BURTON AND COLLIN *with a crowbar, working at the mirror.*

CUT TO

THE MIRROR; *there is a tear and a pop and it swings open and*

CUT TO

ALL THREE *going inside, looking around. The chair, the looted shelves. The truth thuds home.*

RUSSELL *turns, looks out at the bedroom through the door.*

RUSSELL
(dead)
A one way mirror.

Silently, they move out into the bedroom.

COLLIN
— I better get cracking on that license number —

RUSSELL
(no anger now)
— it's all we've got — and <u>he's</u> got the <u>letter opener</u> — blood, fingerprints — Jesus, think what he can do —

> **BURTON**
> *(a powerful man who speaks softly)*
> — the man is a <u>thief</u> — a thief who witnessed a <u>murder</u> —
> *(gesturing around)*
> — it looks like he stole a whole bunch of money — I'll tell you what he's going to do.
> *(beat)*
> He's going to run like hell.
> *(and on that —)*

CUT TO

THE SADDEST EYES YOU EVER SAW.

It's the next morning and LUTHER is back at the same old stand, looking at El Greco. The other art students are there too. So are the suburban housewives.

Everything is as it was — calm and peaceful —

— now a MUSEUM GUARD moves into the doorway, scanning the room.

CUT TO

LUTHER — a quick glance over, then back to his sketchbook —

— and from that glance it's clear all is <u>not</u> calm and peaceful — he's aware of everything in the room.

THE GUARD turns to leave.

Edgy, LUTHER still works away.

THE GUARD leaves.

LUTHER gets set to do the same.

CUT TO

RED, alone in his empty bar, sipping coffee. It's before the place has opened for the day.

LUTHER comes in the back. RED slides the videocassette over, LUTHER pockets it.

> **RED**
> Jordan beat us at the end.

LUTHER

Bad night.

(and on that)

CUT TO

A YOUNG WOMAN PARKING HER CAR — a high rocky area above the Potomac. Below, a jogging path is visible, full of runners.

THE YOUNG WOMAN gets out, locks her car, starts down a narrow walk toward the joggers.

SHE'S IN HER MID THIRTIES. A good face. And there's something familiar about her.

CUT TO

LUTHER, standing by the edge of the jogging path, studying the runners. Now he registers something: and smiles.

CUT TO

THE WOMAN IN HER MID THIRTIES as she comes jogging along. She runs well.

CUT TO

LUTHER. An imperceptible straightening of his clothes.

CUT TO

THE JOGGER. We realize who she is: the little girl in the photo on LUTHER's dining room table. All grown up. Now her face registers something: his presence. Her eyes go down to the path, she increases her speed.

CUT TO

LUTHER. Waving, calling out.

LUTHER

Kate.

(she runs on)

<u>Kate.</u>

(she slows, hesitates, stops)

CUT TO

KATE, hands on hips, breathing deeply, moving to the edge of the path as he approaches. The river flows behind them. Runners pass by.

Beat.

> **LUTHER**
> Probably too late for me to take it up.
> *(she says nothing — he gestures
> toward the path)*
> The jogging.

> **KATE**
> Ahh.

Beat.

> **LUTHER**
> Dumb way to start this, I guess.

Beat

> **LUTHER**
> Wanted to talk to you.

> **KATE**
> About?

> **LUTHER**
> Believe it or not, the weather.
> *(she waits)*
> Nights are starting to get cold.

> **KATE**
> That happens this time of year.

CUT TO

LUTHER. He speaks quickly now, his voice low.

> **LUTHER**
> I was thinking of maybe relocating. Someplace with a kinder climate.
> *(nothing shows on her face)*
> I just wanted to check it out with you first...

> *(still nothing)*
> ... you're the only family I've got.
> *(and on that)*

CUT TO

KATE. She speaks quickly now, her voice low.

> **KATE**
> Luther, you don't have me.

The last words in this world he wanted to hear. But you can't tell from looking at him.

> **KATE**
> You were in prison, remember? You're talking to the only kid during show and tell who got to talk about visiting day.

> **LUTHER**
> This move — I'm talking permanent, you understand.

> **KATE**
> We don't see each other anyway — we haven't seen each other since Mom died and that's what, more than a year?
> *(a step toward him)*
> Look, you chose your life. You had that right. You were never around for me. Well, fine. But I have no plans to be around for you.

And now she stops, turns away toward the path —

— LUTHER can say nothing, watches her —

— then she spins back —

> **KATE**
> *(louder now)*
> — wait a minute — you're lying about something, aren't you? —

> **LUTHER**
> — no —

> **KATE**
> — are you active again? — is that why you're here <u>now</u>?

LUTHER

—no—

KATE moves in close now —

                          KATE
— I don't believe you —
                          (big)
— Christ, Father, <u>what have you done</u>?
                    (and on those words —)

CUT TO

CHRISTY SULLIVAN'S BODY.

*We're back in the master bedroom but now there is a lot of police activity —
people work around the corpse. The place is covered with black fingerprint pow-
der.*

*SETH FRANK moves into the room — Bogart at 40. Chief Homicide Detective
of Middleton County, Virginia but he had a decade of top work in New York
City. Bright, funny, and tough enough for anything you want to throw at him.*

*He kneels beside the body next to an OLDER MAN. This is the MEDICAL EXAM-
INER, fat and bored. SETH studies CHRISTY; sadly shakes his head.*

                          SETH
Christy Sullivan?

                    MEDICAL EXAMINER
                          (nods)
Wife of Walter — most likely came home and stumbled onto a
burglary —

                    WOMAN'S VOICE (over)
— some burglary.

CUT TO

*LAURA SIMON. LAURA is early 30's, and the best lab technician SETH has ever
known, and he knew some good ones in New York.*

> **LAURA SIMON**
>
> I wish my carpets were this clean. And there aren't many prints.

> **SETH**
>
> You serious, Laura?

> **LAURA SIMON**
> *(bewildered)*
>
> It's like Mary Poppins was here.

> **SETH**
>
> Could someone have let him in?

> **LAURA SIMON**
>
> Sorry, Seth, but the entire Sullivan household went to Barbados two days ago.

> **SETH**
>
> Thank you for your continuing support.

> **LAURA SIMON**
>
> Wait— it gets worse —
> *(moving to the door)*
> — the shots came from here. If she interrupted a burglary, she should have been here —
> *(moving to the bed now)*
> — she was killed where she is — all the blood patterns indicate that. But she was looking toward the bed — what in hell was she looking at?

CUT TO

SETH *says nothing as he and* LAURA *go in the vault.* SETH *stares at the chair.*

> **LAURA SIMON**
>
> Looks like someone sat here — but I couldn't find any prints.
> *(lowering her voice, indicating the*
> *one way mirror)*
> You think Sullivan holed up in the chair and watched his wife perform?

> **SETH**
>
> I hope not —

(shakes his head)
— he's such a great man.
(moves back into the bedroom)

CUT TO

THE BEDROOM. *Another* COP *is working on the wall by the bedtable where a hole the size and shape of a bullet is visible.*

                          SETH
                  (as he moves past)
Careful digging that out.
                  (the COP *nods)*

                MEDICAL EXAMINER
                  (by the body)
Looks like he tried to strangle her.

                          SETH
So he tried to strangle her, <u>then</u> went to the door and shot her from behind?

                MEDICAL EXAMINER
                     (beat)
He also inspected her vagina.

CUT TO

SETH. *Stunned.*

                          SETH
He did what? Why?

                    LAURA SIMON
Maybe he couldn't remember if he fucked her.

                          SETH
                   (has to laugh)
A strong burglar with a weak mind — obviously another open and shut case . . .
                  (as he stares around, baffled —)

CUT TO

A HIGH RISE BUILDING.

It's in a different part of Washington than we've seen thus far. Afternoon now.

AN OLD SALESMAN TYPE is trudging into the building. He's slumped, carries heavy salesman type suitcases. He wears a battered hat. As he goes inside —

CUT TO

THE MAIL AREA. THE SALESMAN is opening a slot with the name HAWTHORNE on the outside. A good bit of mail, most of it unsolicited. HAWTHORNE pockets it, unlocks the foyer, heads toward the elevator.

CUT TO

THE ELEVATOR AND HAWTHORNE slowly getting out, heading toward a corner apartment, taking out some keys —

— there are three locks on the door and as he takes out keys —

CUT TO

THE APARTMENT AS HAWTHORNE walks in, puts the suitcases down, flings his hat toward a long sofa —

— it's LUTHER and this, we will come to learn, is what he keeps as his safe house. It's neatly furnished, modern and clean.

Now he moves quickly —

— first he opens a suitcase — it contains his full backpack from the robbery —

— then he opens a locked closet door, revealing a very large and sophisticated safe. As he begins to work the dial —

CUT TO

— the TV on in the living room as he slides the video cassette RED gave him into his machine. Everything has been put away.

CUT TO

THE TV AS MICHAEL JORDAN is introduced to the crowd —

LUTHER sits, nurses a beer, watches intently . . .

CUT TO

AN OLD MAN SILENTLY WEEPING.

This is WALTER SULLIVAN, one of the giants of the era. A self-made billionaire. Remarkably, the man has few enemies.

At 80, his body may be betraying him — he was once handsome — but his mind is that of a young man.

We've seen him before — in the wedding picture on the wall of his mansion. With his young bride CHRISTY.

He is with her again now, at the morgue. A sheet covers her body. The toe tag is visible. WALTER, shattered and desolate, stares at her once joyous face.

PULL BACK TO REVEAL

SETH FRANK, studying WALTER through a one way mirror. SETH is moved at the depth of the old man's grief. Anyone would be. Now, as WALTER slowly rises —

CUT TO

SANDY LORD waiting in an ante room as WALTER enters . . .

SANDY LORD is WALTER SULLIVAN's lawyer. He is 60, abrasive, powerful.

SANDY moves to WALTER, gestures toward the front door. SETH appears through another door, intercepts them.

> **SETH**
> Mr. Sullivan? — I'm Seth Frank, senior homicide detective for Middleton County —

> **SANDY LORD**
> *(protectively)*
> — my client is in no mood for conversation, sir.

> **WALTER SULLIVAN**
> It's all right, Sandy —
> *(looks at SETH)*
> — you're in charge of the case?

SETH
(nods)
I have to ask some questions, but it can be tomorrow.

WALTER SULLIVAN
You want what, positive identification? Yes, that was my wife.
Anything else?

SETH
(notebook in hand)
You'd been in Barbados for two days?

WALTER SULLIVAN
(nods)
I took the entire staff down — always do this time of year.

SETH
But Mrs. Sullivan didn't come.

WALTER SULLIVAN
She was, had it all planned, but you know women, they change
their minds.
(to SETH, softly)
I'd been married to my Rebecca for forty-seven years and when
she died, I decided I never wanted that pain again. One thing I
knew about Christy: she was going to outlive me.

SANDY LORD
I think that's enough for today.
(taking WALTER's arm)

SETH
(beat)
I have to ask about the vault.
(and on that —)

CUT TO

WALTER. *Holds to SANDY for a moment, then lets go.*

WALTER SULLIVAN
You mean the <u>contents</u> of the vault, of course —

(turns to SANDY)
— Sandy, you go on, I'm all right.
(SANDY looks at him a moment)
Really. Go to the reception — obviously I can't make it, but I'm
sure everyone will understand.

SANDY nods, exits. SETH AND WALTER are alone.

Beat. Then —

WALTER SULLIVAN

I know it's not the contents —
(SETH embarrassed, stands there)
You mean the chair. You have to ask about the chair.

SETH
(soft)

Yessir, I do.

WALTER SULLIVAN

But why? Are they connected?

SETH

I think someone sat in it — and I think that someone may have
seen the murder.
(beat)
You were my father's hero, Mr. Sullivan, I promise you this won't
make my highlight reel.

WALTER. CLOSE UP. Humiliated.

WALTER SULLIVAN

I'd hoped I could satisfy her...but you know...and she had
needs and she didn't want to go behind my back...she suggested
the chair...she hoped I might get to like sitting there...
(beat)
...I didn't...

SETH

You don't have to explain.

> **WALTER SULLIVAN**
> *(so hard for him)*

I do, don't you see, I wasn't always like this, I didn't used to need to just watch — don't you laugh, but I was handsome once.

> *(softer)*

I've tried for eighty years to live a decent life. I've given a billion dollars to charity. If this comes to trial, none of that will be remembered — I'll just go out as the joke of the world.

CUT TO

SETH. *He closes his notebook.*

> **SETH**

I'll try not to bother you unless it's absolutely necessary.

> **WALTER SULLIVAN**
> *(beat)*

Will you listen to me whine? Please forgive me, Mr. Frank. I understand. Bother me all you want — do your job.

> *(beat)*

And I'll do mine.

WALTER *slowly moves to the door.* SETH *watches him. Sadly . . .*

CUT TO

A GORGEOUS SHOT OF A VERY FAMOUS PLACE: THE WHITE HOUSE.

The sun is setting. It all looks magical.

CUT TO

A RECEPTION ROOM, *filled with well dressed men and women. Formal attire. The rich and the famous. But the only one we recognize is* SANDY LORD, *deep in conversation with several other men. Now, someone says his name.*

> **MAN'S VOICE** (over)

Sandy.

> *(Sandy turns)*

Is there anything I can do?

SANDY LORD

Mr. President.

(and on those words)

CUT TO

THE 44TH PRESIDENT OF THE UNITED STATES. He has all the natural charm in the world. He is a remarkably bright man, with a phenomenal memory. He is also, at this moment, one of the most popular men in American history, three years into a brilliant first term, a shoo-in for re-election when that ritual comes.

His name, by the way, is ALAN RICHMOND, and we've seen him before, most recently lying drunk in the back seat of a limousine.

CUT TO

RICHMOND

Take a walk with me.
                    (he and SANDY start out of the
                    room. A well-dressed woman moves
                    with them. She is Chief of Staff
                    and her name is GLORIA RUSSELL)

TWO MEN IN SUITS follow behind. BURTON AND COLLIN are their names and they are the best the Secret Service has to offer.

CUT TO

THE GROUP, as it leaves the room, comes to a wide corridor.

RICHMOND
(to SANDY)
Tell me about Walter — how is he? —

SANDY LORD

Eighty and alone, Mr. President.

RICHMOND

He understands officially my hands are tied?

SANDY LORD

Mr. President, he's touched at your concern.

RICHMOND
Any news of the killer?
(SANDY indicates "no"—)
<u>Well, why isn't there</u>? Who's in charge of the case.?

SANDY LORD
Top man — eight years homicide work in New York. But I understand how you feel — it's hard to be patient.

RICHMOND
(terribly upset)
<u>No one</u> understands how I feel — I'm supposed to have all this power but I can't help my oldest friend — more than any man alive Walter Sullivan put me here — and now when he most needs me . . .
(turning to RUSSELL — urgently)
Dammit, Gloria, you're Chief of Staff — your job is to provide solutions —

GLORIA RUSSELL
— I'll get with the Attorney General in the morning, Mr. President —

RICHMOND
— that idiot will just try and cover his ass —
(frustrated)
— how can I show Walter how I truly feel? — he needs to know that —
(now, he has it)
— forget the Attorney General — I'll do it myself —
CUT TO

RICHMOND. CLOSE UP. *On fire —*

RICHMOND
— I'll hold a press conference —and I'll have Walter come —
<u>and I will embrace him before the world.</u>

SANDY. *Listening. Moved.*

> SANDY LORD

He'll treasure that, Mr. President. What a generous gesture.
Thank you. Thank you.
> *(and he reaches out, shakes*
> *RICHMOND'S HAND, squeezes*
> *RICHMOND'S ARM and —)*

CUT TO

RICHMOND — *suddenly* <u>screaming</u> *in pain* — SANDY *pulls back, shocked.*
RICHMOND *looks embarrassed.*

> RICHMOND
> *(quick smile)*

Damn tennis elbow is killing me.
> *(and on that —)*

CUT TO

RICHMOND, *immediately after, and he sure isn't smiling now* — *he storms to-*
ward the Oval Office, RUSSELL, BURTON *AND* COLLIN *hurrying to keep up*

CUT TO

THE OVAL OFFICE *as* BURTON *opens the door for them, closes it once they're in-*
side.

> RICHMOND
> *(throws off his jacket, turns on RUSSELL)*

This thing's worse, Gloria, I need to see a doctor.

> RUSSELL

The country would have to be informed, Mr. President.

> RICHMOND

What happened to <u>my</u> right to privacy?
> *(rolls up his sleeve, studies his cut)*

I'm telling you, goddam Christy nicked a tendon.

> RUSSELL

Burton says it's a flesh wound —

> **RICHMOND**
> *(to BURTON)*

— when did you become such an expert, Bill? — ever been wounded? —

> **BURTON**
> *(quietly)*

Yes, sir. Many times.

CUT TO

THE FIREPLACE. RICHMOND goes to it, rubs his arm, stares at the flames.

> **RUSSELL**

Are you serious about that press conference, Alan?

> **RICHMOND**

Shit yes — media will eat it up.

> **RUSSELL**

Shall I bring Mrs. Richmond home for it?

CUT TO

RICHMOND, turning from the fire now — quietly.

> **RICHMOND**

I think Mrs. Richmond's efforts to help the poor in Asia should not be interrupted.
> *(takes a breath, starts to button his shirt)*

We know anything yet?

> **RUSSELL**

We checked his license plate — he stole the car from a police impoundment lot.

> **RICHMOND**
> *(breaks out laughing)*

Damn, I like the sound of that.
> *(gestures toward his jacket —*
> *RUSSELL helps him into it)*

Has he initiated contact?

> RUSSELL

Burton doesn't think he will.

> RICHMOND

I agree.
> *(checking himself in a mirror)*

Sorry about my behavior — won't happen again; think of it as a blip on the screen. And as far as I'm concerned, so is he.

> RUSSELL

He could be a little more than that, Alan — he <u>saw</u>.

CUT TO

RICHMOND. *Big.*

> RICHMOND

He saw <u>nothing</u> — a drunk woman who liked rough sex too much. He's a burglar. What in hell can he say? And who's going to believe him anyway?
> *(beat)*

Shit, it's not like he had evidence or anything...
> *(and on those words)*

CUT TO

THE LETTER OPENER.

LUTHER holds it. He's in his safe house. It's the middle of the night. LUTHER turns the weapon over and over in his big hands...

CUT TO

THE WHITE HOUSE PARKING LOT. A little later. BURTON is alone in his car, driving home. He turns onto the main road.

He picks up speed. Glances around — no cars are following.

CUT TO

BURTON reaches into his pocket, takes out a microcassette recorder, flicks it on.

> RICHMOND (over)

What happened to <u>my</u> right to privacy?

(beat)
I'm telling you, goddam Christy nicked a tendon.

BURTON *clicks the cassette off, puts it back into his pocket. Drives into the night* . . .

CUT TO

A STOVE WITH ONE BURNER ON HIGH.

A TEA KETTLE is over the flame.

We are in KATE'S TINY KITCHEN *and it is morning and she is clearly not fully awake. She is finishing making instant coffee with lowfat milk and sweet n' low; next she goes to the front door of her apartment, opens it, picks up the morning Washington Post.*

She unfolds the paper as she starts back to the kitchen —

CUT TO

THE WASHINGTON POST.

HUGE HEADLINES *— as big as you can get without a war.*

WALTER SULLIVAN'S WIFE MURDERED

KATE *looks at it only a moment, shakes her head, then starts to turn her attention to another section of the paper —*

— she doesn't get that far.

CUT TO

KATE: *she has seen something she didn't catch before —*

CUT TO

THE FRONT PAGE AGAIN. *And the headline is still there —*

— but there is a smaller headline beneath it:

Jewel Thief Sought

CUT TO

KATE as she sits down hard. Trying for control. Entering a nightmare. She stares at the paper.

CUT TO

THE FRONT PAGE. Pictures of the mansion, of WALTER smiling on his wedding day, of CHRISTY.

But KATE's eyes keep coming back to the smaller headline:

<u>Jewel Thief Sought</u>

She tries to sip coffee, spills. She closes her eyes —

— in the kitchen, the pot of water starts to <u>shriek</u>.

KATE does not move.

CUT TO

A MIDDLE CLASS SUBURB.

Kids riding bicycles. Very Norman Rockwell. Early afternoon.

CUT TO

A BALD MAN. There is the sound of a click. We realize after a moment that the bald man is LUTHER.

Another shot of LUTHER looking very different — full beard. Again, a click.

LUTHER again — elegant beard this time. Click.

PULL BACK TO REVEAL

We are in the basement game room of one of the suburban homes. High school pennants on the walls.

But our attention is on a whole string of Polaroids of LUTHER.

Two people are present: LUTHER AND VALERIE. VALERIE is very small, and doesn't miss much. She has been photographing him, and as the last photo slides out of the camera, she blows on it, puts it alongside the others.

> **VALERIE**
> *(they study the pictures)*
> You always did disappear good, Luther.

> **LUTHER**
> You mean I've got a weak face. Thanks, Val.

> **VALERIE**
> You're lucky is all — some of my customers, they stand out no matter what.

CUT TO

AN ORDER FORM BOOK. *VALERIE licks a pencil with her tongue.*

> **VALERIE**
> How many passports you need?

> **LUTHER**
> *(thinks)*
> Four should cover it.

> **VALERIE**
> *(writes this down)*
> Now you'll want different looks, and matching international driver's licenses — I'll throw in some dummy credit cards, seeing it's you. How the rugs I made you holding up?

> **LUTHER**
> They're good. Beards and mustaches too.

> **VALERIE**
> *(pleased)*
> I try to give value for money. Leaving the country permanent?

> **LUTHER**
> It may come to that.

> **VALERIE**
> Matter where you've been? — I hate doing those goddam Asian passport stamps.

                         LUTHER
Europe's fine. Maybe the Caribbean for winters. When can I
pick up?

                         VALERIE
Overtime's hard nowadays what with the kids being so nosy —
goddam highschoolers — have to charge a ton.
                    (LUTHER nods — it's okay)
I'll put everything else on hold.

CUT TO

VALERIE. She puts the order book down, studies him.

                         LUTHER
What?

                         VALERIE
I don't want to know what you're into, but leaving forever . . .
                         (beat)

                         LUTHER
Finish it.

                         VALERIE
Thirty percent of my runners kill themselves within five years.

                         LUTHER.
                    (kisses her forehead)
Five years doesn't sound so bad to me just now.
                    (and as he heads out)

CUT TO

*SETH AND LAURA in the good sized criminal lab at Police Headquarters.
Loaded with up to date equipment.*

*SETH has drawn the crime scene on the floor in chalk. Words like "Bedroom
Door," "Exit Window," "Vault," "Bed," "Victim" are written neatly to scale.
He holds a sheaf of papers.*

*It's late afternoon and things are already getting crazed. Noise in the back-
ground throughout.*

SETH

See if any of this makes sense.

SETH mimes opening the "Bedroom Door," stepping inside, closing it. He makes a click with his tongue.

SETH

I am Christy Sullivan and I walk in and surprise a burglar.

SETH moves to the "Vault Door," mimes closing that, makes a grunt.

LAURA

Now you're the burglar coming out of the vault and being surprised.

SETH

Gold star.
                    (aims his finger like a pistol)
I draw my gun —

LAURA
                    (cutting in)
— then why do you bother to strangle her when you could just shoot? —

SETH

— that's nothing — why do I bother to have her strip and then put her clothes back on?

LAURA

There I can help you — see, before you were a burglar you were a society dry cleaner and you still love beautiful clothes.

SETH

And I dress her because?

LAURA

She was a good customer and you didn't want her embarrassed when the police came.

CUT TO

SETH. CLOSE UP. Frustrated.

SETH

She had a point .21 blood alcohol level — she was too drunk to drive. I've checked every cab and limo company in the area and not one of them knows anything. Someone drove her home. Goddamit, who?

CUT TO

AN OPEN DOOR BEHIND THEM. A TELEPHONE REPAIRMAN appears. Nice looking kid with a dazzling smile.

TELEPHONE REPAIRMAN

Lieutenant? — sorry to bother you —
                    (SETH turns)
— I've got your phone working again, shouldn't give you any more trouble.

SETH

Good service, thanks.

TELEPHONE REPAIRMAN
                    (dazzling smile)

Part of the job.

                    (as he goes —)

CUT TO

SETH AND LAURA. SETH's lost his train of thought.

SETH

Oh yeah — remember that bullet hole in the wall? — had the lab dig out the slug — guess what —no slug — why does the burglar take the time to do that?

LAURA

Different from the one in her body?

SETH
                    (getting more and more upset)

Oh I like that a lot — two different guns means two different burglars. Two guys broke in? And they both went out the window? Bullshit.

(*big*)
Why does he go out the window in the first place when he got in by breaking a zillion dollar security system? —

COP (over)

Seth?

SETH
(*whirling*)

What?

COP
(*in the doorway*)
A Bill Burton of the Secret Service in the parking lot.

SETH
Oh right, he said he'd stop by.
(*gives the papers to LAURA*)
Here, you solve the goddam thing.
(*as he starts away*)
I hate this case — I really truly hate this case — you cannot imagine how much I hate it —

CUT TO

THE PARKING LOT.

BURTON *waits by his car as* SETH *walks up.*

BURTON
(*as they shake*)

Bill Burton, hi —

SETH

— hi, Seth Frank —

BURTON

— I know you must be going crazy — but the boss is very interested in your progress. Maybe we can help each other.

SETH

What can I do you guys can't?

BURTON

You know Sullivan and the President are like father and son?

(SETH nods)

The minute anything breaks, if you'd call me, I'd tell the President. That way, he'd be the first to alert Mr. Sullivan — and I can help you by giving you top priority — on anything.

(takes out a card)

Here's my numbers.

He turns, opens his front car door.

BURTON
(getting in)

Leads?

SETH

Still trying to figure out what might have happened —

BURTON

— I loved playing Sherlock Holmes.

SETH
(surprised)

You Secret Service guys do that?

BURTON

I was State Trooper here ten years before the Government got me.

CUT TO

SETH. *It just pops out.*

SETH

You're <u>that</u> Bill Burton.

CUT TO

BURTON. *Embarrassed.*

BURTON

I was younger and dumber then.

(quickly)

Keep in touch.

(SETH waves as BURTON drives away)

CUT TO

BURTON. *He drives alertly along, turns a corner. Up ahead, a telephone repair truck has stopped. THE REPAIRMAN leans out. He has a dazzling smile. He and BURTON wave to each other . . .*

CUT TO

A BEAUTIFUL DINING ROOM.

Quietly elegant. TWO MEN *are finishing dinner. WALTER SULLIVAN we know.*

MICHAEL MCCARTY, *his dinner companion, is 35, fit, handsome, beautifully dressed. He is at present torn by a silver tray of small French pastries.*

There is, it might be noted, a mild hum in the background.

> WALTER SULLIVAN
> *(noting MCCARTY's temptation)*
> The chef makes them especially for me — I promise you they're sinful.

MCCARTY *grabs one, downs it, grins sheepishly.*

> MCCARTY
> You're a salesman, Mr. Sullivan.
> *(SULLIVAN nods, and as they rise —)*

CUT TO

THE LIVING ROOM. *Tastefully appointed, as one would expect.*

What comes as something of a surprise is that we can now tell where we are — strolling through one of WALTER SULLIVAN's private planes — which explains the motor hum.

This particular private plane, it might be noted, is a 747. *It seems to go on forever.*

> WALTER SULLIVAN
> You have a flawless reputation, Mister McCarty — which is why
> I need to employ you.

MCCARTY

Understood.

WALTER SULLIVAN

I have no idea who I'm after. Until I do, you will have to wait in Washington for instructions.

MCCARTY

Out of the question, I'm afraid.
(*explaining as they walk along*)
Mine isn't particularly creative work — I only do it because I enjoy living beyond my means. I can't afford to just sit around.

CUT TO

A SOFA. WALTER gestures for them to sit.

WALTER SULLIVAN

When I was 10 my father died — he was a miner and lung disease killed him. I became rich at 25 and the first thing I did was purchase that mine, close it, and give every miner who worked there fifty thousand dollars to retire on.
(*beat — staring at MCCARTY now*)
You will come to Washington, Mister McCarty. You will choose a penthouse suite, and I will put one million dollars expenses per week into the Swiss bank account of your choosing.
(*beat*)
And, when the time comes, two million dollars a bullet.

MCCARTY
(*smiles, nods*)
You are a salesman, sir.

WALTER SULLIVAN

Selling sin is easy . . .
(*now sharply —)*

CUT TO

CLOSE UP. An old mug shot of LUTHER.

PULL BACK TO REVEAL

SETH and LAURA, in his office. The mug shot is on his desk, along with some folders. And a short fax.

SETH

Who is he?

LAURA

Luther Whitney —
(the words tumble out)
— got here early, this fax came, no number, just says to check out Luther Whitney. Crank note, right? — but what else do we have? nothing, so I hit the computer and his name came up and it was interesting so I called a girlfriend at the Bureau to do a quick check —
(really excited)
— Seth, listen — this is one of the great thieves of the world.

SETH
(dubiously)
Why haven't I ever heard of him?

LAURA

Because he hasn't been arrested in thirty years.

SETH. For the first time now, intrigued.

SETH

And they kept his file <u>highlighted</u> all that time?

LAURA

I didn't say he hasn't been <u>questioned</u> — just nothing sticks. Bureau says only half a dozen people could pull off the Sullivan job. I'm running checks on the others —
(beat)
— but Whitney lives in Washington.

SETH

That's not evidence —
(fingering the mug shot)
— and this sure looks like he's been arrested —

                              LAURA

— in the old days — he's a three time loser — but he was working with other guys then — now he always works alone.

                              SETH

And yesterday you were convincing me there were two gunmen,
which doesn't fit. What else doesn't fit?

                              LAURA
                          (reluctantly)
He hasn't killed in forty-five years.
                              (beat)
Korea.

                              SETH
                          (looks at her)
You nuts? — you telling me to go harass a war veteran? — Jesus,
he's probably living on his social security.

                              LAURA

Worse than that — a <u>wounded</u> veteran. Combat. Decorations.
Lives on his disability. <u>Says</u> he does.
                              (excited)
I'm telling you, he's our guy —

                              SETH

In the first place, how do we know he's so great if he never gets
caught? —
                              (glum)
— and I don't do war heroes ...

CUT TO

LUTHER — *it's a beautiful morning now and he's walking up the steps to the
art museum.*

He seems in a terrific mood and as he goes inside —

— HOLD.

SETH *has been on the steps of the museum, watching him. Now quickly —*

CUT TO

LUTHER, *inside, peering back out at* SETH. *And he doesn't seem in as terrific a mood now. He hesitates, keeps on going and*

CUT TO

SETH. *Outside — and he knows* LUTHER *was watching.*

CUT TO

EL GRECO. *The usual group has gathered, sketching away.* LUTHER *is deeply engrossed in his labors.*

CUT TO

SETH, *entering the room, casually taking it all in. He approaches the group, ends up behind* LUTHER *who is intent on getting the hands right.*

> **LUTHER**
> *(not looking)*
Boy, you must be smart.

> **SETH**
> *(really taken aback)*
Sorry?

> **LUTHER**
Usually it takes a week for you guys to get to me.
> *(turns, smiles)*
You look just like your picture, Seth, I'm Luther Whitney.
> *(and as he reaches out to shake a
> surprised* SETH's *hand —)*

CUT TO

THE MUSEUM COFFEE SHOP *as they walk in, go to the food line. There is, throughout, a bantering tone. Not that it matters but these two, in a different world, would like each other — they're both, in their own ways, deeply moral men.*

> **LUTHER**
So do you want my confession now or after coffee?
> *(draws some coffee from an urn)*

                            SETH
                        (doing the same)
Before I send you away for life, I should probably check out your
alibi.

                            LUTHER
Watched the Bullets game with Red Bransford. Prison buddy of
mine — runs a bar — want to question me about the game? I'm
probably lying.
                    *(they each give the cashier some
                        money and we)*

CUT TO

A QUIET TABLE IN THE CORNER as they head for it.

                            SETH
You been following the case?

                            LUTHER
                        (nods vigorously)
I love true crime —

                            SETH
 — FBI feels only a few could have handled something as hard
as the Sullivan.
                    (touches his notebook)
I've got a list here; you're on it.

                            LUTHER
Honored.

                            SETH
Truth is, someone sent a fax implicating you.

                            LUTHER
                        (nothing shows)
I wish it was true.
                        (shakes his head)
Your robber actually went <u>in</u> the front door but came <u>out</u> down
a rope in the dark in the middle of the night?

                    (SETH nods; LUTHER sighs)
If only I could do stuff like that — I'd be the star of my AARP
meetings.

CUT TO

LUTHER AND SETH as they sit. SETH smiles, looks at LUTHER.

                         SETH
                         (beat)
Luther? — why was it so hard?

CUT TO

LUTHER. Now he's surprised. He kind of smiles.

                         LUTHER
You want <u>me</u> to help solve your case?

                         SETH
Just looking for insight. How would you — scratch that — how
would <u>one</u> go about it? What kind of person do you think I
should be looking for.

                         LUTHER
                       (like a shot)
Older fella. Like me.

                         SETH
                     (now he smiles)
Because?

                         LUTHER
Need patience. The secret is just research, research, research —
from everything I've read.

CUT TO

*SETH. This hasn't gone at all the way he thought — and he's starting to get
fascinated.*

                         SETH
Research for what?

                                    LUTHER
Well, from what I can tell on the tube, it's not an old house.
                                (SETH nods)
There had to be an architect, right? You'd be able to tell which
one from public records in the library. And once you know the
office, you could break in and find the plans and xerox them, get
them back before morning.

                                    SETH
Not just steal them?

                                    LUTHER
Seth —breaking in isn't hard —what's hard is breaking in so no
one knows anyone's been there. Now, after the architect, next
you'd want the contractor's office — and the security company's
office.
                                    (beat)
You know the skill involved breaking the security of a security
company?
                                (shakes his head)
I wonder how those guys do it?

                                    SETH
Why go to all that trouble?

                                    LUTHER
Papers said he kept the money in a vault, yes?
                                (LUTHER nods)
Well, I'm guessing there was probably some secret way to open
it —

                                    SETH
                                (casually)
— clicker —

                                    LUTHER
                                (fascinated)
— explain —

                                    SETH
— gizmo — looked like a VCR programmer —

LUTHER
(shaking his head)
— amazing what science comes up with —
(beat)
— must have been a lot of money inside.

SETH
(sipping casually; a pause)
Five million.

(and on those words —)

CUT TO

LUTHER, *more than he thought, a* <u>lot</u> *more — but of course nothing shows —
instead he breaks out laughing.*

SETH

Why's that funny?

LUTHER

The way you said it — as if you were trying to surprise me.

SETH
(smiles)
I was trying to surprise you.

LUTHER
(smiles back)
There you go.

CUT TO

SETH. *He sips his coffee, takes out his notebook, opens it.*

SETH

Now is this disguises business really true?

LUTHER

Seth, you've got to get with the program you expect to catch this
guy — mostly likely it is a guy, am I right? Some kind of weird
loner?

SETH

Maybe like you.

LUTHER
(couldn't agree more)
I'm the perfect prototype.
(sipping away)
But you see any face often enough, you'll start putting things to-gether. That's why these top guys disguise themselves. I read a great article a couple of years back — damn, I wish I could re-member where — anyway, it was about these make-up experts some of them use — wigmakers, people like that.

SETH
(flipping a page)
Go on about these wigmakers.

LUTHER
I'd love that but I'm late as it is — got to get my pacemaker checked —
(he likes Seth)
—all this excitement, you understand.

SETH
(and he likes LUTHER)
A) you don't have a pacemaker, and B) I'll be back tomorrow.

LUTHER
Tomorrow is promised to no one.
(HOLD ON LUTHER)

CUT TO

LUTHER IN THE BEDROOM OF HIS SMALL HOUSE —

he is throwing clothes into a suitcase while talking on the phone —

LUTHER
Not 'til morning? —
(makes a face)
— I'll be by early —
(beat)
— no, Valerie, I can't wait 'til your kids are off to school —
*(hangs up, shuts the suitcase, takes
off out the door —)*
CUT TO

A PLACE WE'VE SEEN BRIEFLY BEFORE — KATE'S APART-MENT.

Dark. Moonlight through the windows.

The sound of a key in the door.

LUTHER enters, takes out a tiny flashlight. We're in one large-ish room, books all over. The home of someone who doesn't care a whole lot about their home.

CUT TO

THE TINY KITCHEN AS LUTHER enters. He opens the fridge. Disaster — still water, sparkling water, carrot sticks.

> **LUTHER**
> *(sadly, muttering)*
> Katie darling, you've gotta try <u>food</u> sometime.
> *(he closes the door, moves back into*
> *the room —)*

CUT TO

A GRADUATION PHOTO OF KATE. LUTHER touches it with a fingertip, moves on through the silence.

CUT TO

LUTHER by the bed now, he flashes his light around —

CUT TO

—what the light illuminates: a bed table full of law books. Expected. A phone/answering machine. Expected. The mandatory lamp.

And photographs. A PROUD MOTHER AND DAUGHTER PICTURE. THE DAUGH-TER is KATE. THE MOTHER is a fine looking woman with a kind face. Half a dozen more shots as KATE grew up, THE MOTHER grew older. MOTHER AND DAUGHTER, MOTHER AND DAUGHTER. Nothing unusual here at all.

So why is LUTHER so sad?

HOLD.

CUT TO

OUTSIDE MIDDLETON COUNTY COURTHOUSE.

10 A.M. A white brick, weather-beaten building, Old Glory. fighting the breeze.

> RICHMOND (over)
> I am having this press conference here because . . .

CUT TO

RICHMOND, speaking on a podium. The press corps stands in front of him, TV crews of all kinds, CNN the most noticeable.

> **RICHMOND**
> . . . it is here, at Middleton County Courthouse, that Christine Sullivan's killer will be tried for his crime.

CUT TO

BURTON AND COLLIN, in the background, scanning the crowd. GLORIA RUSSELL stands behind them.

CUT TO

THE SAME SHOT — only now it's grainy — we're watching it on a TV screen. CNN. Now —

CUT TO

AN AIRPORT LOUNGE. CNN on the tube. A BARTENDER cleaning glasses; otherwise, not a whole lot going on.

Now LUTHER enters, dressed for travel. He goes to a stool, orders a ginger ale, puts his passport and ticket on the bar, glances toward the TV.

> **LUTHER**
> Turn that off, okay?

> **BARTENDER**
> *(finishing up the glasses)*
> In a sec.

CUT TO

RICHMOND at his press conference. He speaks without notes and he speaks beautifully.

RICHMOND
Of course you heard endlessly during the last campaign that I came from an impoverished family in an impoverished town and how, in spite of everything, we lived with our doors unlocked.

CUT TO

RUSSELL watching, listening; she loves hearing him talk.

RICHMOND (over)
We <u>all</u> lock our doors now, but that is not what concerns me ...

CUT TO

BURTON AND COLLIN, scanning the crowd.

RICHMOND (over)
... <u>we are also locking our hearts</u> ... <u>that</u> is the sadness, <u>that</u> is the loss.

CUT TO

RICHMOND, and suddenly he's like a Southern minister.

RICHMOND
We are locking our hearts to the cries of the weary, we are locking our hearts to the pain of the poor ...

CUT TO

AN OLD MAN, standing behind RUSSELL. We realize it's WALTER SULLIVAN.

RICHMOND (over)
... Sisters and brothers, we are locking our hearts to ourselves.

CUT TO

WALTER SULLIVAN. Grainy now. CNN. He has aged shockingly in the past couple of days.

CUT TO

LUTHER, in the airport lounge, staring sympathetically at the devastated old man.

— SULLIVAN's image suddenly is gone —

THE BARTENDER has turned off the television.

> **LUTHER**
> *(politely)*

Put it back on.

> **BARTENDER**
> *(starting to argue)*

You said —

CUT TO

> **LUTHER**
> *(cutting through)*

<u>Do it</u>—

CNN. WALTER SULLIVAN is still there.

> **RICHMOND** (over)
> <u>We feel savagery and violence must be allowed a place at table.</u>
> *(beat)*
> That is wrong. That is not America. I shall fight that battle.

CUT TO

LUTHER, staring at the image of WALTER SULLIVAN, who is heartsick and beaten. LUTHER is simply transfixed —

CUT TO

RICHMOND on CNN and now he has turned and is beckoning for WALTER SULLIVAN to join him.

SULLIVAN for a moment is uncertain. He points to himself — "do you mean me?" RICHMOND nods, opens his arms out wide. SULLIVAN gets up, comes forward.

CUT TO

LUTHER, *as he gets up too, also comes forward, leaving the stool, walking close to the television.*

CUT TO

RICHMOND AND SULLIVAN, *grainy on CNN as* RICHMOND *embraces* SULLIVAN, *holds him in a loving embrace.*

RICHMOND
Dear friend, old friend, <u>we</u> shall fight that battle.
(SULLIVAN, *too overcome by the*
moment, can only nod)
Who can explain the ways of chance? If we had never met, I would not be President. If Christine hadn't taken ill, she would have been with you in Barbados and we would not be here. Oh Walter, I would give the world to lessen your pain.

CUT TO

THE PRESS CORPS. *Subdued, saddened.*

CUT TO

RICHMOND AND WALTER. *They turn, face the cameras.* THE PRESIDENT'S *arm is still around the* OLD MAN; *they both blink back tears and now,* <u>now</u> —

— <u>*here it comes!*</u> —

CUT TO

LUTHER IN EXTREME CLOSE UP. *Tears of rage in his eyes. A rage so deep it shocks him —*

LUTHER
You — heartless — prick —
(*building*)
— <u>you — fucking — bastard</u> —

CUT TO

THE BARTENDER, *surprised, turning toward* LUTHER. *He starts to say something, stops; something tells him to shut up and he does.*

CUT TO

RICHMOND, wiping away tears, alone on camera.

CUT TO

LUTHER, wiping away tears, in the bar.

CUT TO

A SHOT OF THE TWO OF THEM, LUTHER AND RICHMOND, one on CNN, one in reality, because LUTHER has moved so close to the TV he and RICHMOND could almost be staring at each other.

LUTHER

I'm not running — not from you.

(big)

I'm going to bring you down!

HOLD ON the two men in tears.

CUT TO

SEVENTY VERY EXCITED PEOPLE WE'VE NEVER SEEN BEFORE.

They stare around at their surroundings —

— THEY ARE IN THE WHITE HOUSE. ON A GUIDED TOUR.

In the Green Room more specifically.

A bright late morning of what's going to be a beautiful day.

A GUIDE leads the PEOPLE through a doorway.

They troop happily along.

LUTHER is with them; he seems happy too.

CUT TO

THE STATE DINING ROOM.

A knockout.

THE GUIDE leads THE PEOPLE through. They look around, chat with their friends, follow THE GUIDE out.

LUTHER follows THE GUIDE out too.

HOLD ON THE DINING ROOM.

All is as it was.

Except a large envelope has been dropped on a side table.

MOVE IN ON THE ENVELOPE —

— it's addressed to GLORIA RUSSELL. Now, quickly —

CUT TO

GLORIA RUSSELL. *Terrified.*

We are in RUSSELL'S OFFICE IN THE WHITE HOUSE. The doors are closed, RUSSELL is at her desk. BURTON stands alongside. COLLIN, silent, sits in a corner.

And on her desk, half out of the envelope, is a photograph of the letter opener.

> RUSSELL
IIe was in the building — son of a bitch took a guided tour.

BURTON pulls the picture all the way out, studies it.

> RUSSELL
I've never dealt with blackmail —

> BURTON
> *(trying for calm)*
— he doesn't want money —

> RUSSELL
> *(exploding)*
— you a fucking mind reader?

> BURTON
> *(under control)*
No, I just looked on the back —
> *(shows her)*
— see? —
> *(a small piece of paper is taped there)*

CUT TO

RUSSELL
(grabbing it, reading)

"I don't want money."

CUT TO

RUSSELL is more upset. BURTON almost smiles.

BURTON
(admiringly)

This guy sure has the guts of a burglar. Wish we had him.

(COLLIN laughs)

RUSSELL

You finished your recruiting speech? Because I'd sure like to know how I handle this.

BURTON

Like you handled the letter opener?

CUT TO

RUSSELL. She studies BURTON. Then —

RUSSELL

Gee, Bill, that could be construed as criticism. Do you really want me as an enemy?

CUT TO

BURTON. He stands there, massively powerful. His voice, when he speaks, is his usual voice: polite, considerate.

BURTON

Miss Russell, I should have called the police that night. But I was weak. You convinced me to stay silent. I regret that.

(another pause)

Know this: every time I see your face I want to rip your throat out.

CUT TO

RUSSELL. Silence. Then she shrugs.

RUSSELL

Fine – you win the pissing contest —
(beat)
— but don't we have to do <u>something</u>?

BURTON
(shakes his head)
<u>No</u> — because he's making a terrible mistake — he thinks he has
<u>time</u> — he doesn't — Seth Frank's too good. He'll bring him in.

RUSSELL

Then what?

COLLIN
(his first words)

Then I kill him.

(now, from them —)

CUT TO

KATE IN HER OFFICE.

She is, we will find, a top prosecutor for the Commonwealth of Virginia. Her office is a zoo.

On her desk, a baby picture of KATE AND HER MOM smiling — but there is something a little different about it.

CUT TO

SETH as he enters and they shake. He glances around —

— sees the photograph, glances away.

KATE has risen now — and in the silence it's clear that even though they are both standing still, they are both circling.

SETH
(trying for a smile)
For a tough prosecutor, you don't resemble your reputation,
Miss Whitney.

                              KATE
                           (the same)
Is that good or bad?
                    (before SETH can reply)
Look, Lieutenant — I told you on the phone, I'm simply not involved with my father, so this may not be a waste of time for you,
but it sure is for me.

                              SETH
What would you do if I just turned around and left?

                              KATE
Report you as an incompetent.

                              SETH
                       (a real smile now)
You're <u>exactly</u> like your reputation, Miss Whitney —
                        (as they head out)

CUT TO

A LOUNGE as they enter. It's empty.

                              SETH
                  (the instant they're alone)
I'm assuming you sent the fax.
                     (KATE says nothing)
And I'm also assuming you're very involved with your father —

                              KATE
— why for God's sakes? —

                              SETH
— you think it's all coincidence? He's a thief and you just happen to be the toughest prosecutor in the area?

                              KATE
                        (just amazed)
Wow — that never crossed my mind — you think there might
be some connection? — like maybe I'm somehow compensat-
ing? — I better write that down.

SETH

Luther disappeared.

(no reaction)

CUT TO

A BANGED UP COUCH. KATE sits, shrugs.

SETH

I think you can help me.

KATE

Lieutenant — I don't know the man — he was in jail when I was a kid, when he got out my mother and I went off to live by ourselves. We don't make contact. He doesn't care about me. I've seen him all of once this past year.

SETH

When?

KATE

Couple days ago. He said he might be going away. There. I just helped you. Can I go back to work now?

(SETH shakes his head)

CUT TO

SETH AND KATE. And they realize something. in a different world, under different circumstances, they'd probably be starting an affair.

KATE

(snappishly)

Quit wasting my time — if he doesn't want you to find him, you're not going to find him.

SETH

You saying he's left town, skipped the country, what?

KATE

I'm saying you won't recognize him. I'm saying he could be just around the corner — he always kept a safe house —

> SETH
> *(cutting in)*

— where? —

> KATE

— nobody ever knows —

> SETH

— then where'd you hear all this? —

CUT TO

KATE. CLOSE UP.

> KATE

— my mother loved him, all right? — even after she left him —
even when she was dying she always talked about him — "if only
he hadn't this," "if only he could have that—"
> *(she stops)*

CUT TO

SETH, watching her.

> SETH

And?

> KATE

I meet a lot of asshole cops like you — guys who O.D.'d on
Columbo —

> SETH

 — lady, I may be an asshole cop but you don't know me well
enough to call me one —

> KATE

— there's something else, isn't there? Something you want me to
do? — but you won't say —

CUT TO

SETH. There is. But he won't say.

CUT TO

KATE. *For the first time now, apprehension.*

CUT TO

A ROW OF TINY HOUSES ON A WASHINGTON STREET.

Well tended.

CUT TO

SETH AND KATE *as he parks in front of one of them. She stares at the little place; very apprehensive now.*

> KATE

How long did he live here?

> SETH

Years.
> *(opens the car door)*

Just in and out.
> *(KATE shakes her head)*

It's a murder case, Kate —

> KATE

— in and out.

CUT TO

THE FRONT DOOR. SETH *stoops, gets the key from under the terra cotta planter.*

> SETH

Strange place for a thief to leave a key, don't you think?

> KATE
> *(quick memory)*

He always did that...

CUT TO

THE LIVING ROOM *as they enter. It's surprisingly tidy.*

CUT TO

SETH AND KATE *as they move along. SETH is watching KATE who suddenly stops dead as we*

CUT TO

THE MANTLE. A large blow up of the same picture KATE had in her office, the one of KATE AND HER MOM—

— with one startling change: <u>LUTHER is in this shot</u>, standing there proud and smiling.

She has ripped his presence out of her photo.

CUT TO

SETH, silently watching Kate. She turns sharply away. He gestures for her to follow.

CUT TO

THE BEDROOM as they enter. Clothes tossed all over.

                              SETH
He must have just taken off — what scares a professional thief like that?

CUT TO

KATE. No reply. She has seen something across the tiny room and is drawn to it —

CUT TO

LUTHER'S bedtable —

—<u>and here it is!</u>

Call it a montage, call it a collage, call it what you will, we are looking at dozens of photographs —

— all of them featuring KATE.

Many of them we saw in her apartment — only here, as in the photo over the mantle, LUTHER is there with KATE AND HER MOM.

WE ARE LOOKING AT A SHRINE!

And there are newer photos too — KATE at her college graduation, KATE at her law school graduation, KATE AND HER MOTHER coming out of an elegant restaurant, KATE alone on the steps of Middleton County Courthouse —

— these are not posed shots. She looks wonderful and alive in all of them —

CUT TO

KATE. *She looks dead now. All energy gone. She sits heavily down on the bed.*

> **KATE**
> *(fighting tears)*
> ...but he wasn't at those places...
> *(pointing to the grown up photos)*
> ...college graduation; law school graduation; the night Mom and I celebrated when I got a job; and me alone on the steps? — I'd just won my first case, I was so proud...
> *(still fighting)*
> ...I used to think...sometimes I'd come home and I'd sense he'd been in my apartment, checking the fridge, shaking his head because he never thought I ate right...it's crazy but I just knew Daddy was here...
> *(and now she loses it, starts crying silently)*

CUT TO

SETH. *He kneels alongside her, gives her a handkerchief.*

> **SETH**
> You can do a good thing, Kate —
> *(beat)*
> — help me bring him in. Just leave a message on his phone machine, you're worried about him —

> **KATE**
> ...no...

> **SETH**
> It's the truth — you <u>are</u> worried about him — his life's in danger, you can save him, make the call —

> **KATE**
> ...he won't come...

> **SETH**
> Look at these pictures —

(soft, fast)
Of course he'll come. You're all he has.

CUT TO

KATE, *staring at the photos, trying to get control.*

SETH
(moving in)
Kate, he's on the run and he's scared and he's <u>right</u> to be scared
because he's <u>going</u> to get caught —you don't know the heat on
this case — and what happens if some hotshot who's trying to
make a reputation captures him? —
(beat)
Don't you see, <u>I can guarantee his safety</u>. You make the call, I
make a promise: you'll have your father, home and dry...

CUT TO

KATE *alone in her apartment. Totally wiped out. She is on the phone with*
SETH. *Outside, the sun is dying.*

KATE
I left a message on his machine, he called back within an hour;
we're meeting tomorrow afternoon.

CUT TO

SETH *in his office, taking it down.*

SETH
Where?

KATE (over)
An open air place near my office, the Cafe Alonzo —

SETH's *excited.*

CUT TO

BURTON *in his office, taking it down.*

KATE (over)
— four o'clock — it's deserted then.

BURTON's *excited too.* HOLD.

CUT TO

THE MOON, *high in the sky — middle of the night now.*

CUT TO

KATE. *Wired. Pacing across her small apartment, back and forth, back and forth.*

CUT TO

SETH, *alone in his office, going over plans, sipping coffee to stay awake.*

CUT TO

BURTON, *alone in his bed, staring at the ceiling, a nearly empty scotch bottle in one hand.*

CUT TO

COLLIN, *in bed, fucking his brains out. A* WOMAN *is riding him, wild with passion — it takes us a moment to realize it's* GLORIA RUSSELL.

CUT TO

LUTHER, *in his safe apartment, listening to the phone machine. We hear* KATE'S VOICE. "DADDY . . . I MISS YOU . . . I'M WORRIED . . . CALL ME . . . "*A click.* LUTHER *hangs up, immediately dials again. We hear the message start over.* "DADDY . . . I MISS YOU . . . "

For the first time in awhile, LUTHER'S *on top of the world.*

CUT TO

Early morning — on what's going to be a gorgeous fall day.

CUT TO

BURTON, *yawning, blowing into a steaming paper cup of coffee.* COLLIN, *wide awake, moves alongside.* COLLIN *is carrying a rifle —*

— we are at a government firing range.

CUT TO

COLLIN, *squinting into the morning sun.*

CUT TO

BURTON, *putting down the coffee cup, picking up a pair of binoculars.*

CUT TO

BURTON AND COLLIN *staring out —*

— a distant target is being raised.

CUT TO

COLLIN. *He strokes the barrel of his high-powered rifle.*

CUT TO

THE TARGET. *A long way off.*

CUT TO

BURTON, *as he has focused the binoculars —*

CUT TO

THE TARGET *seen through the binoculars as it comes clear — the bull's eye is small.*

CUT TO

COLLIN *with his rifle. His fingers still move along the barrel. No hurry whatsoever —*

— and then it all goes fast, and in one motion he is aiming and firing and firing again and the sound <u>explodes</u> and

CUT TO

BURTON, *dazed.*

CUT TO

THE TARGET —

— the bull's eye has been totally blown away.

CUT TO

BURTON AND COLLIN. BURTON *puts the binoculars down,* COLLIN *puts the rifle down — and no question,* COLLIN'*s flying —*

CUT TO

A DOWNTOWN MEN'S STORE. LUTHER AND A SALESMAN *are engaged in conversation.* LUTHER *is buttoning a new raincoat to the throat.* THE SALESMAN *holds several hats.* LUTHER *picks one, tries it on.*

> **LUTHER**
> I need to look really good today. Make an impression.
> *(doesn't like the hat)*

> **SALESMAN**
> Business?
> *(*LUTHER *tries the other hat —*
> *very rakish, he likes it)*
> It's a woman, I can tell.
> *(*LUTHER *nods)*
> Never too late, is it?

CUT TO

LUTHER. *Beaming.*

> **LUTHER**
> You got that right.
> *(now, from his happy face —)*

CUT TO

THREE CURSING WORKMEN.

PULL BACK TO REVEAL

A MODERN OFFICE BUILDING. THE WORKMEN *are on a scaffolding two stories up, struggling to replace a glass panel that has cracked.*

THE GLASS PANEL *is heavy and bulky and* THE WORKMEN *are having a bitch of a time with it.*

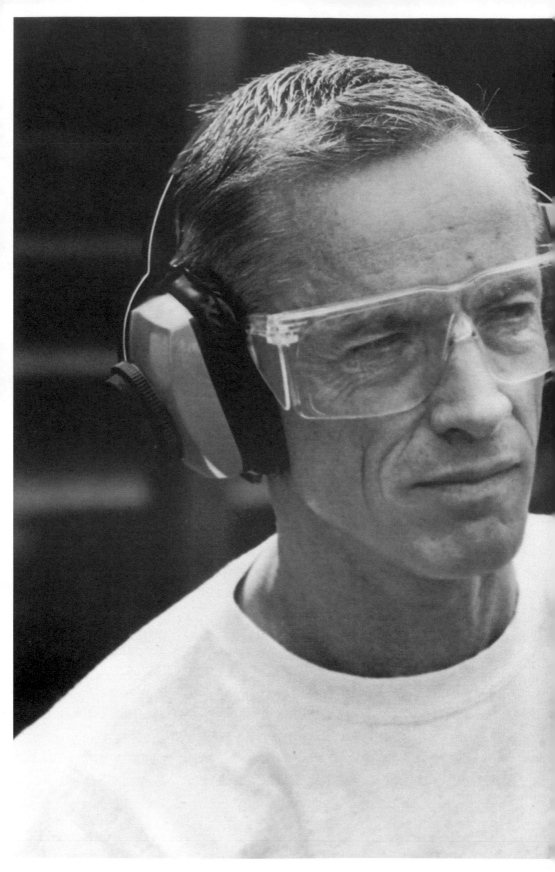

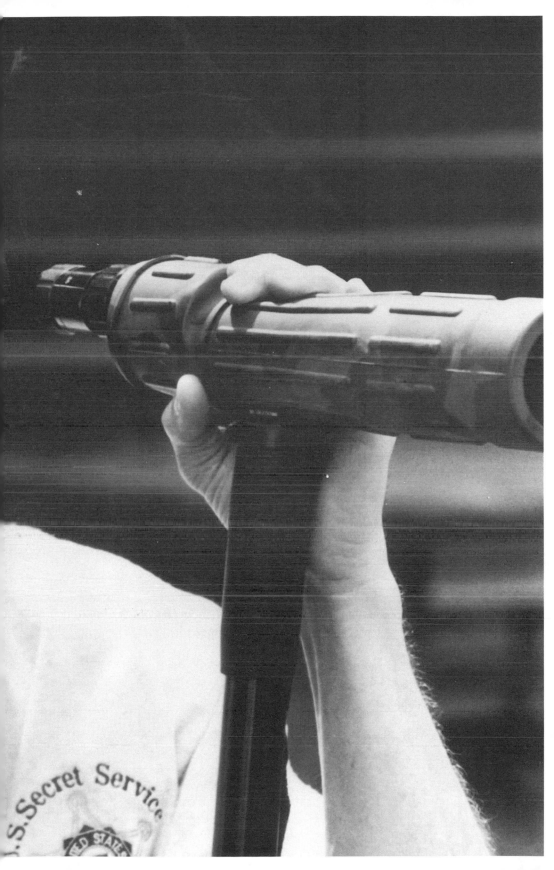

THE ENTIRE FRONT OF THE BUILDING IS GLASS PANELS. It mirrors the area across the street — a bunch of dilapidated brownstones.

CUT TO

THE BROWNSTONES. They are empty and, according to a sign, are due for demolition. All the windows of the brownstones are closed — except one. On an upper story.

CUT TO

Inside the window. MICHAEL MCCARTY, who we last met on Walter Sullivan's 747, is there. He looks out.

CUT TO

HIS VIEW. The glass building and the struggling WORKMEN and, on the ground floor, a few tables are set outside, with large umbrellas alongside each.

There is a sign: CAFE ALONZO.

CUT TO

MCCARTY. Beside him is a leather case. He opens it.

CUT TO

THE CASE. A VERY HIGH POWERED RIFLE. MCCARTY begins to expertly assemble it, taut and businesslike.

CUT TO

SETH, taut and businesslike, in his headquarters. He stands by a blown-up map of the Cafe Alonzo area. The restaurant is circled — and around it are marked places for policemen to wait — SETH is giving instructions to those policemen now—

— fifty of them. And no one's smiling.

CUT TO

KATE in her apartment. Dressed and ready. Lying on her bed. Afternoon now. She gets up, makes it halfway to the front door —

— can't do it — she turns, goes back to the bed, lies down again, frozen.

CUT TO

THE CURSING WORKMEN. *The glass panel is so damn cumbersome they are having a miserable time.*

CUT TO

THE CAFE ALONZO. AN ELDERLY COUPLE *sits at one of the half dozen outdoor tables. Finished, they rise, walk away.*

The place is empty.

CUT TO

SETH, *outside headquarters now, giving instructions to police officers. Behind them: two dozen unmarked cars.*

CUT TO

THE SUN. *Later in the afternoon.*

CUT TO

BURTON, *getting out of his car at* SETH's *Police Headquarters.*

CUT TO

SETH, *finishing instructing a couple of dozen* MOTORCYCLE COPS. BURTON *moves up behind* SETH, *waits quietly. As* SETH *is done, he sees* BURTON, *they nod, start toward* SETH's *car.*

BURTON
The Boss is very grateful for this.

SETH
Figured he might like an eyewitness report of the capture.

THE THREE WORKMEN. *Making some headway with the bulky glass panel —*

— now <u>crosshairs</u> cover them and we

PULL BACK TO REVEAL.

MCCARTY, *staring out the window of the brownstone, the rifle pointed — very relaxed, he pulls the trigger —the rifle's not loaded yet — and the staccato "click" is all we hear.*

CUT TO

SETH AND BURTON *moving quickly into the lobby of the glass office building that adjoins the Cafe Alonzo — the lobby has a clear view of the outdoor part of the Cafe.*

Around and behind them, DOZENS OF COPS *get in position.*

CUT TO

Around the corner from the glass building — unmarked cars.

CUT TO

MOTORCYCLISTS, *waiting in shadow, out of sight.*

CUT TO

SETH AND BURTON. *They've both seen a lot — which doesn't mean they're not tense.* BURTON *takes out some Tums, offers them to* SETH. SETH *shakes his head, brings out Tums of his own.*

CUT TO

THE SUN. *Starting down.*

CUT TO

THE THREE WORKMEN *and they hate their job. One of them glances down and we*

CUT TO

THE CAFE ALONZO. *Empty.*

Now, from THE WORKMEN'S *angle,* A WOMAN *moves to one of the tables. It's* KATE. *They don't pay much attention.*

CUT TO

KATE. *She hesitates, then decides on the front table. She takes a breath. Sits. Motionless.*

CUT TO

KATE.CLOSE UP —

— now <u>crosshairs</u> cover her face and we

PULL BACK TO REVEAL

McCarty as before, with his weapon. He pulls the trigger again and again there is the "click" — now he flicks away a grain of dust from the barrel —

— then he puts the weapon down, reaches out and we

CUT TO

One bullet. <u>It's supersonic ammo</u>. McCarty picks it up, blows on it gently. He might be holding a child.

CUT TO

Burton and Seth. They can see Kate sitting alone in the late afternoon. Now Seth mutters "fuck" and — a goddam <u>Waiter</u> has appeared and is walking out toward Kate. He is Asian and very young.

CUT TO

Kate, startled as The Waiter calls out from behind her.

> **WAITER**
> Miss?
> *(Kate spins around)*
> What you want please?
> *(his English could be a lot better)*

> **KATE**
> Nothing, thank you.

> **WAITER**
> Got to.

> **KATE**
> Pardon?

> **WAITER**
> *(gesturing)*
> You sit you eat please.

CUT TO

SETH AND BURTON. Stunned.

SETH
This is not part of my brilliant master plan.
(more Tums)

BURTON
Unfuckingbelievable.

They both crunch away.

CUT TO

MCCARTY, watching the WAITER and KATE. He's not happy either. He points a finger at the WAITER, goes "Boom."

CUT TO

KATE, and it's almost four o'clock and she's not at her best.

KATE
(gesturing around)
I'm waiting for someone.

WAITER
He must eat too, please.

KATE
Oh he will, we both will — we'll order half the menu — <u>but just not now</u> —

CUT TO

THE WAITER nods, finally he turns, starts off.

CUT TO

KATE. Trembling.

CUT TO

THE WAITER, returning.

WAITER
Cheesecake gone.

KATE

Thank you so much.

THE WAITER nods again, and this time he does go.

CUT TO

KATE, watching him, making sure. Now she sits straight —

CUT TO

KATE. CLOSE UP. Very shaky, trying to hold it together. And now <u>crosshairs</u> cover her face as we

PULL BACK TO REVEAL

COLLIN. He holds a very high-powered weapon. It looks like it could kill from a thousand yards away.

CUT TO

WHERE HE IS — and it's not a thousand yards away — he's in an unmarked van on the street, even closer than MCCARTY.

CUT TO

COLLIN, loading his weapon. His movements are skilled. His concentration is total.

CUT TO

MCCARTY, glancing out at the office building area. THE THREE WORKMEN on the scaffolding are fighting to right the glass panel. one of them grabs a rope connected to a block and tackle.

He pulls on the rope.

Slowly, the piece begins to rise.

CUT TO

KATE, sitting alone, studying her hands.

CUT TO

SETH AND BURTON. The waiting is agony.

CUT TO

KATE. *It's worse for her.*

She glances around —

— nothing, no one

CUT TO

McCARTY. *All the time in the world.*

CUT TO

COLLIN. *Blows on his weapon slightly.*

CUT TO

KATE, *and it's a question of how much longer she can take it. Her trembling is almost out of control — she glances around again and —*

— and there he is!

CUT TO

LUTHER WHITNEY *himself, and he looks splendid in his new raincoat and hat —*

— he moves along in the shadow of the office building, toward the Cafe, walking with his usual grace — LUTHER *always seems to glide.*

CUT TO

McCARTY *in the window. Spotting* LUTHER *— totally controlled.*

CUT TO

COLLIN *in the van. The same.*

CUT TO

SETH AND BURTON *and the instant* LUTHER *is visible,* SETH *gestures toward the* POLICEMEN: Get ready.

CUT TO

McCARTY, *raising his rifle.*

CUT TO

COLLIN, *raising his.*

CUT TO

THE THREE WORKMEN, *raising the glass panel.*

CUT TO

KATE. *Watching her father come closer.*

CUT TO

LUTHER. *It's hard to suppress a smile as he walks toward his daughter.*

CUT TO

KATE, *watching him come.*

CUT TO

LUTHER, *almost there. Speaks softly.*

LUTHER
I did not kill that woman, Kate.

CUT TO

McCARTY, *flipping off the safety.*

CUT TO

COLLIN, *doing the same.*

CUT TO

LUTHER AND KATE, *and he starts to sit —*

CUT TO

SETH, *right hand raised — he's about to start it all in motion.*

CUT TO

McCARTY, *his finger floating to the trigger.*

CUT TO

COLLIN, *doing the same.*

CUT TO

LUTHER, *seated now and as at last he reaches out for his daughter's hand* —

CUT TO

— THE THREE WORKMEN, *and for a moment the glass panel slips and tilts and as it catches the afternoon sun* —

CUT TO

— MCCARTY, *blinded as the red reflection hits his eyes but he* <u>fires</u> *and*

CUT TO

LUTHER AND KATE *as suddenly the umbrella at their table is* <u>severed</u> *and starts to topple and*

CUT TO

COLLIN, *startled, and he fires too and*

CUT TO

LUTHER, *instantly diving toward* KATE *as the second bullet explodes in the pavement close by and*

CUT TO

SETH, *stunned, because this is crazy and*

CUT TO

BURTON, *stunned, eyes wide and*

CUT TO

LUTHER, *taking* KATE *down to the sidewalk, protecting her body with his body and* —

CUT TO

Madness! — because it all goes nuts now as there are shouts and screams and people running this way, that way

— SETH is in the center of it all, shouting instructions, racing with BURTON out of the building —

— unmarked cars fill the street —

— a hundred uniformed policemen charge —

— motorcycles roar in from everywhere —

— KATE lies dazed — staring at the chaos — here come _fifty_ uniformed policemen —

— and here come _fifty more_ —

— McCARTY races out of the back of the building, leaps into a sports car, guns away —

— COLLIN disassembles his rifle, scrambles from the van —

—— BURTON stays close to SETH, watching it all

— THE THREE WORKMEN look down at it all   then they look at each other in total confusion — _what the fuck is going on?_ —

because what they see is that the recently deserted plaza is now _stuffed_ with cops and more cops and vehicles and here come more and here come even more —

— and KATE sits now, staring around, looking for LUTHER —

— and SETH in the middle of it all stares around, looking for LUTHER

— _because where the hell is he?_ —

CUT TO

A BLACK POLICE LIEUTENANT, shouting for his men to spread out and

CUT TO

BURTON, turning, turning, trying to make sense of it all and

CUT TO

THREE POLICE SERGEANTS ON MOTORCYCLES gunning through the crowd and

CUT TO

KATE, standing now, looking down — <u>and then she sees it</u> —

— on the ground where LUTHER was: <u>a new raincoat and a new hat</u> and —

CUT TO

SETH, and it's all gone wrong and it's all going crazy and there is noise and there are shouts and there are whistles and

CUT TO

THE BLACK POLICE LIEUTENANT, breaking into a run, chasing after someone we can't quite make out and

CUT TO

A TALL UNIFORMED POLICE LIEUTENANT, entering the CAFE ALONZO —

— he passes a couple of guys in chef's hats and a CHINESE WAITER who just gapes out toward what was his service area —

— THE TALL UNIFORMED POLICE LIEUTENANT moves gracefully past —

— it's LUTHER.

He goes to the front door of the place, glances back toward where the noise is still mounting —

— shakes his head —

— out the door and gone!

CUT TO

THE DOOR TO KATE'S APARTMENT OPENING

and SETH coming in with KATE. Evening. KATE is as drained as you'd expect.

KATE
(glancing around)

Messy.

                              SETH

I like that in a woman.
                    (she doesn't smile)

CUT TO

SETH, giving her back her keys and a piece of paper. His voice is raw from all the shouting.

                              SETH

Top number's local police —
                       (she nods)
— other two are my office and home.
                     (another nod)
I live alone too, call anytime. Want me to get someone to spend the night?

                              KATE

I just need some sleep.

                              SETH

I've got surveillance outside. And I'm keeping it on til this is over. I've got a feeling he's going to try and contact you.

                              KATE

You're on a hot streak, I guess.

                              SETH

Listen, I'm sorry.

CUT TO

KATE. Nothing to say.

                              SETH

Anything unusual, call me right away — not a bother, I live alone.

                              KATE

You said.

                              SETH
                      (he knows that)
Feeble, huh?

(she nods)

CUT TO

THE TWO OF THEM. *They look at each other. Then he starts toward the door. Slowly.*

> **KATE**
>
> Anything for the road? I've got water and water.

> **SETH**
>
> Deal.

CUT TO

THE KITCHEN *as they enter and she opens the fridge —*

— and it's full of food: milk and fruit and cookies. KATE *stares, then quickly glances at* SETH. *He just points to a bottle.*

> **SETH**
>
> Pelligrino would be great.
> *(KATE can't help it, breaks out laughing)*
> What's funny, I say it wrong?

> **KATE**
>
> Tired is all.
> *(as she hands him a bottle —)*

CUT TO

THE FRONT DOOR *as they move toward it. He opens it.*

> **SETH**
>
> I don't think I've told you this but I live alone.
> *(and this time she does smile. And
> he does go)*
> Lock it behind me.

> **KATE**
> *(locking it loudly)*
>
> How's that?

> SETH (over)
>
> Real good. Try and sleep.
>> *(his footsteps get softer, disappear)*

> KATE
>> *(still facing the door, her back to*
>> *her apartment)*
>
> I betrayed you twice, Luther, you better know that now.

> LUTHER (over)
>
> Not the first to do it.
>
>> *(as KATE turns)*

CUT TO

LUTHER, *standing there, looking at her.*

> KATE
>
> Why'd you come?

> LUTHER
>
> You have to know I'm not a murderer.

> KATE
>
> No, this afternoon. Why'd you come then? You must have sus-
> pected something, or you wouldn't have been prepared.

> LUTHER
>> *(simply)*
>
> My daughter wanted to see me.
>> *(points to the couch — as KATE sits)*

CUT TO

LUTHER, *and before she's even seated, he's into it.*

> LUTHER
>
> The robbery went fine 'til they came in. Hid in the vault. They
> were drunk. Sex got rough. He was going to kill Christy, but she
> turned the tables, was going to kill him. Two guys came in, shot
> her dead.

> KATE
>
> The same two guys tried for you this afternoon?

LUTHER

I think maybe only one of them. Walter Sullivan could have hired the other.

KATE

Pretty powerful enemy, good going.

LUTHER

Not as powerful as Alan Richmond.

KATE just looks at him. Dead silence.

LUTHER

Richmond was the drunk. The two guys are Secret Service. Chief of Staff Russell planned the cover-up.

KATE just looks at him. Dead silence.

CUT TO

LUTHER. Studying her. Not a great reaction.

CUT TO

KATE. Little shake of the head.

LUTHER

Every word true.

KATE

You saying you're innocent of the murder?
(*LUTHER nods*)
Then you must go to the police. That's what innocent people do.

LUTHER

I'm a three time loser — I can't spend my last years in jail.

KATE

Why in the world should I believe you?

LUTHER. CLOSE UP. Long pause.

LUTHER

Because I swear on Mattie's grave.

CUT TO

KATE, <u>rocked</u> —

CUT TO

LUTHER, going to her

CUT TO

> **LUTHER.**
> <u>On your mother's grave, Kate</u> — you know I'd kill myself before I lied about that.

KATE. Looking at him. Because he wouldn't lie, not about that. Everything he's told her, all true.

The air goes out of her.

Silence.

> **KATE**
> *(soft)*

Jesus, Luther.

> **LUTHER**

I know.

> **KATE**

They'll kill you.

> **LUTHER**

I know.

> **KATE**

Can you run?

CUT TO

LUTHER as he sits beside her on the couch.

> **LUTHER**
> I was set to. At the airport. All the money I needed to go anywhere I wanted to go.

CUT TO

LUTHER. CLOSE UP.

> **LUTHER**
> But I saw that prick using Sullivan on the TV — I maybe could-
> n't have saved that woman, Kate. <u>But I didn't even try</u>.
> > *(beat)*
> I know what you think of me and I know what we've been to
> each other —
> > *(beat)*
> — <u>haven't</u> been to each other. And it's not the time to try and ex-
> plain my life —

CUT TO

KATE, watching his face now.

> **LUTHER**
> — but I've never robbed anyone couldn't afford it and I've never
> stiffed a waitress.
> > *(beat)*
> And Alan Richmond has to pay.

> **KATE**
> What can you do?

> **LUTHER**
> Not a whole lot maybe — but I know I only went to jail when I
> had partners.
> > *(beat)*
> People betray each other, Kate — nowadays, when there's a
> group, someone wants to write a book —
> > *(beat)*
> — <u>These people hate each other</u>. And if I can drive them just a
> little bit nuts, they might make a mistake.
> > *(rises now)*
> And if they do, I'll be there.
> > *(looks at her)*
> Glad for the talk, wish we'd had more.
> > *(and he starts to go)*

CUT TO

LUTHER *crosses to the door, turns.*

> **LUTHER**
> This is probably it; you understand that.
> > *(she does — he still looks at her. Then —)*
> I was never going to tell you this, but I watched you argue a case
> last year — thank God you got your brains from your mother.

> **KATE**
> > *(she's standing now too — they're*
> > *across the room from each other)*
> It's dangerous outside.

> **LUTHER**
> It always is —
> > *(beat)*
> — and I may not make you proud, Kate
> > *(soft)*
> — but I'm not going down alone...
> > *(and on that)*

CUT TO

AN ELEGANT HIGH RISE IN WASHINGTON.

Crisp cool afternoon. A DOORMAN *stands outside, enjoying the day.*

A WELL DRESSED MAN *round the corner; he holds a small, beautifully wrapped package with a small envelope attached. He moves to the* DOORMAN.

> **WELL DRESSED MAN**
> > *(it's* LUTHER*)*
> For Miss Gloria Russell.
> > *(hands it over)*

> **DOORMAN**
> > *(taking it)*
> Want me to sign anything?

> **LUTHER**
> I trust you.

(and he turns, walks quickly away
as we —)

CUT TO

THE ENVELOPE *being opened. It's early evening now and* RUSSELL *is in her apartment. The message inside is short and clear —*

"*Gloria,*
Thanks for the rescue.
Alan"

RUSSELL *smiles, and as she opens the package —*

CUT TO

A BEAUTIFUL NECKLACE. *Antique most likely. And tasteful —*

— we hear the sound of an orchestra playing waltzes.

PULL BACK TO REVEAL

GLORIA RUSSELL, *looking just splendid, the necklace around her throat, entering a large and very impressive White House dinner-dance. Clearly an important affair of state.*

We've never seen RUSSELL *quite like this — relaxed, secure in her femininity. She nods distantly to* BURTON AND COLLIN *who are, as always, close to* THE PRESIDENT. *For the first time now we realize something:* GLORIA RUSSELL *is hot for* ALAN RICHMOND.

CUT TO

RICHMOND, *on the edge of the dance floor, chatting with some elderly couples, several of them European, all of them wealthy.*

RICHMOND
(as RUSSELL *approaches)*
You're a vision this evening, Miss Russell.

RUSSELL
Thank you, Mr. President.
(beat)
And thank <u>you</u>, Mr. President.

> **RICHMOND**
(doesn't understand)

For?

> *(radiant, she indicates the necklace)*

Come again?

> *(this time she touches it — he bends
close to her)*

> **RUSSELL**
(whispering)

You sent it to me this afternoon.

> *(long pause — then)*

CUT TO

RICHMOND. CLOSE UP. *So* happy.

> **RICHMOND**

Well of <u>course</u>.

> *(now, to the others)*

Excuse me, all — I am overcome with the desire to dance with my Chief of Staff.

> *(a hand to her — RUSSELL,
beaming, moves out onto the dance
floor with him)*

CUT TO

EVERYONE at the gathering, watching them.

CUT TO

RICHMOND AND RUSSELL, very much aware that all eyes are on them —

— what we don't know is this: they are both <u>wonderful</u> dancers. And they seem to be reveling in their moves — because throughout this they never stop smiling.

> **RICHMOND**

What in hell are you talking about?

> RUSSELL
> (*surprised*)

Your gift, Alan — I was overwhelmed — and your note was so gratifying —

> RICHMOND
> (*cutting in*)

— I sent a note?

> RUSSELL

Yes, yes, you think I don't know your writing? I assumed you wanted me to wear it tonight.

CUT TO

THE NECKLACE. *He looks at it as they spin gracefully.*

> RICHMOND

It is lovely, Gloria — and you know what else?
> (*they do a perfect dip*)

> RUSSELL

What, Alan?

> RICHMOND

Christy Sullivan wore it the night she was killed.

CUT TO

RUSSELL, *a quick glint of panic, a gentle peal of feminine laughter.*

CUT TO

RICHMOND AND RUSSELL — *he bends her back, their mouths are close.*

> RICHMOND

You know what this means? — Whitney's been heard from at last.

CUT TO

RUSSELL. CLOSE UP. *They spin and glide. Long pause. Then —*

> RUSSELL

It's not precisely the first time, Mr. President.

CUT TO

RUSSELL. *The music is building to climax now.*

Their movements become more grand.

> **RICHMOND**
> *(so happy)*
> You've been keeping things from me, is that what you're saying?

> **RUSSELL**
> Only because you have so much on your plate, Alan; we wanted
> to spare you.
> *(beat)*
> He did send me a Polaroid of the letter opener yesterday.

CUT TO

RICHMOND. *CLOSE UP. A kick in the teeth —*

— he summons all his control, goes into even more complicated movements.

CUT TO

THE CROWD OF ELEGANT MEN AND WOMEN — *it's really wonderful dancing
they're seeing — they start to applaud.*

CUT TO

RICHMOND AND RUSSELL, *hearing the sound.* RICHMOND *acknowledges it with
a smile as they come to climax.*

> **RICHMOND**
> Jesus —
> *(a final flourish)*
> — I need time to think — come to my office in the morning —
> *(beat)*
> — This will certainly make an interesting chapter for my mem-
> oirs.
> *(and as they bow)*

CUT TO

THE CROWD, *applauding louder while on the dance floor,*

THE PRESIDENT OF THE UNITED STATES AND THE CHIEF OF STAFF applaud happily back. As the sound builds —

CUT TO

THE THANK YOU NOTE that was sent to RUSSELL.

PULL BACK TO REVEAL

THE OVAL OFFICE.

The papers and the note are on RICHMOND's desk. He studies them. RUSSELL, BURTON AND COLLIN stand silently watching him.

The smell of death's in the room.

> RICHMOND
> *(holding the note now. His voice is,*
> *when he speaks, calm)*
> It's excellent work.
> *(to BURTON)*
> Any idea who could have forged it?

> BURTON
> I talked to Seth Frank — apparently Whitney learned how in prison.

> RICHMOND
> Very gifted man.

CUT TO

THE WINDOW as he walks to it, looks out.

> RICHMOND
> And are we close to stopping him?

> RUSSELL
> We're working just as hard as we can.

> RICHMOND
> Good to know that.

> BURTON
> He'll make a mistake.

>   **RICHMOND**
> Good to know that too.

CUT TO

RICHMOND. CLOSE UP. *With more meaning than the words convey —*

>   **RICHMOND**
> How can we get to this guy?
>   *(pause)*
> I think we all know the answer.

CUT TO

THE OTHER THREE, *looking at* RICHMOND.

CUT TO

>   **BURTON**
> You're sure you want to do that?

>   **RICHMOND**
>   *(nods)*
> She's a young prosecutor, prosecutors ask questions — She
> might know what he knows.
>   *(a reassuring smile)*
> Show you love your country.
>   *(on those words —)*

CUT TO

A GAS STATION ON THE OUTSKIRTS OF WASHINGTON.

Midafternoon now.

LUTHER's *at a pay phone.*

CUT TO

SETH IN HIS OFFICE. *As he picks up the phone —*

>   **LUTHER** (over)
> Kate okay?

                              SETH
  Where are you?

CUT TO

LUTHER. Fast.

                             LUTHER
  I'm not staying on long enough for you to track this, just answer
  me.

CUT TO

SETH IN HIS OFFICE.

                              SETH
  She couldn't be in better hands — talk about catching a break,
  Secret Service called me, they're taking over surveillance —

CUT TO

THE TELEPHONE swinging back and forth —

— and in the background, a car motor roaring away.

CUT TO

KATE, coming down the elevator of her apartment building — she's in her jog-ging clothes now.

CUT TO

LUTHER, on the outskirts of Washington, driving like crazy.

CUT TO

KATE, driving into the park where she jogs.

CUT TO

LUTHER, honking his horn, driving through WASHINGTON, faster than before.

CUT TO

THE ROCKY PARKING AREA HIGH ABOVE THE JOGGING PATH.

Not many other cars so KATE *gets a space in front, overlooking the river, and as she stops, takes out her keys —*

— another car comes roaring in and backends her hard —

— there is a screech of brakes and a scream —

CUT TO

KATE IN HER CAR *as it teeters at the edge and then starts its long fall to the jogging path far below and*

CUT TO

LUTHER, *running through the park —*

— up ahead is the jogging path — above it the parking lot —— and he stops dead, stares wide eyed as we

CUT TO

KATE'S CAR, *careening against a rocky ledge, then cartwheeling the rest of the way down, landing horribly, spinning, finally coming to rest upside down and*

CUT TO

LUTHER, *racing to the car; hands shaking, he manages to pull the front door open and reach inside —*

— now there are cries as other joggers stop and stare and

CUT TO

KATE, *as* LUTHER *pulls her body out of the wreckage.*

LUTHER
(*terrified*)

   ...Katie...?

— no response — it's impossible to tell if she's alive —

— in the distance now, the sound of an ambulance.

CUT TO

THE *AMBULANCE, siren <u>screaming</u>.*

PULL BACK TO REVEAL

Early evening now, getting dark, and the ambulance braking in front of the emergency room of

A LARGE CITY HOSPITAL —

— as doctors and attendants with gurneys come pouring out —

CUT TO

A PRIVATE ROOM. *Later.* KATE *is bandaged and attached to a bunch of equipment —*

— but however faintly her breathing, it's still breathing and it's steady. She's alone for the moment in the semi-darkened room.

CUT TO

An empty corridor outside. A DOCTOR *comes walking along — it's* COLLIN.

CUT TO

KATE *in her room, sleeping. Another* DOCTOR *is with her now, checking her charts.*

CUT TO

COLLIN. *He sees what's going on, stops, pulls out a small notebook, pretends to read it, all the while glancing towards* KATE's *room with the one* DOCTOR *still there —*

— now from around the corner, noise, coming closer — several people approaching, perhaps more.

COLLIN *turns away from the sound, curses, then stops —*

— THE DOCTOR *is done with* KATE's *charts.*

From around the corner now, the group coming closer still.

CUT TO

KATE'S DOORWAY *as* THE DOCTOR *exits and* COLLIN *enters — they pass each other —*

*— * COLLIN *moves a step further into the room —*

—and now there is something in his hand —

— A HYPODERMIC NEEDLE.

CUT TO

KATE. *Out of it. Lying there, eyes closed.*

CUT TO

COLLIN, *the needle ready, moving silently toward the bed.*

KATE *is barely breathing.*

CUT TO

And now suddenly <u>COLLIN</u> *is barely breathing —*

— because THE OTHER DOCTOR'S ARMS *have viced around* COLLIN'S NECK, *forcing the air out of him and*

CUT TO

COLLIN, *stunned, but trying to struggle —*

CUT TO

THE DOCTOR *jerking* COLLIN'S *body into the air — his feet are dangling now —the hypodermic needle drops to the bed as the struggle goes on —*

—— and COLLIN *is in fabulous shape. And he's young and powerful and he's been in terrible situations before and he knows how to fight and he's been taught to defend himself and —*

— and tough shit —

— THE DOCTOR — it's LUTHER — relentlessly increases the pressure against COLLIN's throat —

— COLLIN can't even gasp now —

— his feet can't kick anymore —

— his body starts to go limp —

— his eyes start to slide up into his head —

— silence in the room —

— it's almost over —

— which is when suddenly LUTHER lets go.

CUT TO

COLLIN, eyes flickering open as LUTHER lays him down on the floor. All this next is <u>whispered</u>.

CUT TO

THE HYPODERMIC NEEDLE as LUTHER picks it up carefully.

> **LUTHER**
> Going to guess this wasn't to pep her up.

> **COLLIN**
> *(staring, eyes wide)*
> ...you're not going to kill me...

> **LUTHER**
> ...why do you think that...?

> **COLLIN**
> ...you could have but you didn't...

CUT TO

LUTHER. Kneeling by COLLIN now.

> **LUTHER**
> That's because you didn't know your crime.

— and now he jams the needle into COLLIN's neck.

COLLIN *tries to cry out, but* LUTHER *covers his mouth.*

CUT TO

> **LUTHER**
> *(kneeling close, whispering into*
> COLLIN's *ear)*
> I didn't mind you tried to shoot me at the restaurant — I wouldn't have minded if you'd nailed me at Sullivan's — part of the job —
> *(beat)*
> — but you fucked with blood.

CUT TO

COLLIN. *Dying now. His breathing is getting strange, his body starting to stiffen.*

> **COLLIN**
> ...mercy...

CUT TO

LUTHER, *bending over him.*

> **LUTHER**
> I'm fresh out.
> *(and on that —)*

CUT TO

> **KATE** (over)
> ...Daddy...?

CUT TO

KATE, *eyes barely open. From her position* LUTHER *is simply kneeling, nothing else is visible...*

> **LUTHER**
> ...go to sleep, honey...

(she tries to stay awake, can't make
it, drifts off)

CUT TO

KATE. *She closes her eyes.*

CUT TO

COLLIN. LUTHER *closes his eyes for him. Now —*

CUT TO

A GURNEY *with a figure on it being pushed by* A DOCTOR.

CUT TO

A DUMPSTER OUTSIDE —

— the gurney is there —

— the figure isn't —

— the sound of a car gunning into the night and we

CUT TO

SETH *coming out of the shower in his bathroom. He puts a towel around him, wipes the steam off the mirror, cries out —*

— LUTHER *is standing there.*

> **LUTHER**
> Listen to me — I need one answer — when you interviewed Walter Sullivan, did he say why Christy didn't go to Barbados?

> **SETH**
> *(shakes his head)*
> Just that she changed her mind.
> *(studying* LUTHER*)*
> You know who did it, don't you?

> **LUTHER**
> So will you — check your phones —

SETH
(incredulous)

— who'd tap a police officer?

No reply — LUTHER's already headed for the door as we —

CUT TO

WALTER SULLIVAN getting into his limousine in front of a Georgetown mansion. Later in the evening. The car starts to move. WALTER looks frail and very old now. And somehow smaller.

CUT TO

WALTER huddled in the back seat, as the street lights illuminate him. He might even be ill. In any case, a sad figure.

CUT TO

THE LIMOUSINE, turning a corner.

CUT TO

WALTER. Blinking.

WALTER SULLIVAN

Is this a shortcut home, Tommy?

THE CHAUFFEUR
(turns; it's LUTHER)

I'm your replacement driver for the evening, sir. Don't worry, he's fine.

WALTER SULLIVAN

Very unusual — what do I call you?

LUTHER

Luther, sir.

WALTER SULLIVAN

And are you familiar with how to get to my home, Luther?

LUTHER

I know the way, sir — I'm the man who robbed you —

SULLIVAN says nothing; stares unsmiling.

                         LUTHER
— and you're the man who tried to have me killed —

                    WALTER SULLIVAN
— I'm sorry I missed — I believe in the Old Testament, sir —
there is nothing wrong with an eye for an eye when a terrible
deed has been done.
                          (ice)
A deed such as yours.

                         LUTHER
You want to believe that, don't you? — makes your life a lot sim-
pler if you believe that, isn't that right?
                        (big now)
What do you think I gain being here?

CUT TO

SULLIVAN. Contempt.

                    WALTER SULLIVAN
Have no idea — you going to rob me again? —

CUT TO

LUTHER.

                        LUTHER.
I don't need your money, Mr. Sullivan. Look in your vault lately?

                    WALTER SULLIVAN
                        (he has)
I'm afraid we're a little late for an attempt at leniency.

CUT TO

THE CAR. A SCREAMING TURN.

CUT TO

INSIDE THE CAR.

> **LUTHER**
>
> Shit's coming down tonight, Mr. Sullivan, do you want to be a player or not?
>
> *(bigger)*
>
> Do you want to know what happened, or not? I saw. Your call.

> **WALTER SULLIVAN**
>
> *(beat)*
>
> I want to know.

> **LUTHER**
>
> Are you up to hearing about it?— do you want to hear how he beat the shit out of her and tried to strangle her — you have enough left for that? —

> **WALTER SULLIVAN**
>
> *(a nod)*
>
> — I could walk through fire —

CUT TO

LUTHER, fast now.

> **LUTHER**
>
> I was in the chair when they came in.
>
> *(SULLIVAN says nothing)*
>
> They were drunk — at first he only wanted to bruise her but when she fought back, he went for the kill -- but she turned the tables. Then he screamed for help.
>
> *(pause)*

> **WALTER SULLIVAN**
>
> Who else was in my house?

> **LUTHER**
>
> Secret Service shot her.

> **WALTER SULLIVAN**
>
> *(doesn't like it)*
>
> Nonsense.

> **LUTHER**
>
> Gloria Russell handled the cover up.

> WALTER SULLIVAN

Stop this —

> LUTHER

— don't you want to know who the man was?

> WALTER SULLIVAN
> *(desperate)*

It was <u>you</u>.

> LUTHER

We're too old to bullshit each other, Mr. Sullivan.

> WALTER SULLIVAN
> *(big)*

Who was it then?

> LUTHER
> *(bigger)*

<u>You know</u>!

CUT TO

SULLIVAN, *shaking his head as* LUTHER *roars on.*

> LUTHER

Don't shake your head at me — when you're alone at night, when the <u>rage</u> takes you and you think of what you'd do to revenge her, on those nights <u>you put a face to your enemy</u>.

> WALTER SULLIVAN
> *(coming apart)*

Stop the car —

> LUTHER

— we're going all the way, Walter —

> WALTER SULLIVAN

— it's too terrible.

> LUTHER

It sure is.

CUT TO

WALTER SULLIVAN. A long shaky moment, then —

WALTER SULLIVAN
... of course I know all about Alan's reputation as a philanderer ... but ... he would never dream of betraying <u>me</u> ... I .gave him the Presidency.

CUT TO

LUTHER AND WALTER as LUTHER turns a sharp corner and the wheels scream —

LUTHER
(pressing it)
The press conference — remember? — he held you in his arms and said if only Christy hadn't gotten sick it would have been a different world —
(bigger)
— <u>how do you think he knew she was sick?</u> <u>You</u> didn't tell anybody. And he didn't make it up — he <u>heard</u> it. From <u>her</u>. She told him that's what she'd told you. And I heard every word —

CUT TO

WALTER. For a moment, no reaction. Then he sits back hard. The air's out of him. He just breathes quietly. Then —

WALTER SULLIVAN
That's not real proof.

CUT TO

LUTHER. Handing something back.

LUTHER
And this?

SULLIVAN takes it —

— it's the letter opener.

SULLIVAN leans back, shuts his eyes.

> WALTER SULLIVAN

You could have stolen this.

> LUTHER

I did steal it. But that isn't my blood and those aren't my prints.

CUT TO

SULLIVAN. CLOSE UP. Eyes still shut —

— and he's very old and you expect tears —

— but he didn't get to be WALTER SULLIVAN by crying —

— HOLD ON WALTER —

— and this incredible shriek of rage explodes! —

CUT TO

LUTHER, suddenly stopping the car —

— AND WE'RE IN FRONT OF THE WHITE HOUSE.

CUT TO

WALTER. He sits in the back a moment.

Then he gets out.

LUTHER has gotten out too. They stand close to each other. They nod. Then WALTER starts away.

> WALTER SULLIVAN
> *(turns — quiet now, at peace)*

I did love her, you know.
> *(and he walks away)*

CUT TO

A WHITE HOUSE SECURITY GUARD AS WALTER APPROACHES.

> WALTER SULLIVAN

Is he working late? I haven't an appointment but I'd like to see him if I might.

GUARD
You don't need an appointment, Mr. Sullivan.
(and as he waves him through —)

CUT TO

LUTHER, *standing there, watching the* OLD MAN.

CUT TO

WALTER, *a final turn back, a nod of the head.*

CUT TO

LUTHER. *He nods back, returns to the car, gets in —*

CUT TO

LUTHER *driving through the night.*

CUT TO

WALTER *entering the White House proper.*

CUT TO

SETH, *with a bunch of other officers, standing in front of an office with the name* BILL BURTON *on a plaque — he opens the door —*

— BURTON *has blown his brains out. A note alongside reads:* "*I am so sorry.*" *Alongside the note is a microcassette recorder and a dozen tapes.*

CUT TO

LUTHER. *Driving faster.*

CUT TO

WALTER SULLIVAN *approaching a* METAL DETECTOR *— he starts to go through —*

— it goes off —

— WALTER's *embarrassed. He holds up his wrist, showing his watch.*

THE SECURITY GUARDS *smile, wave him to go ahead.* WALTER *continues on.*

CUT TO

LUTHER, *tense,* ROARING *along.*

CUT TO

GLORIA RUSSELL — SETH *is with her — he cuffs her, leads her out —*

CUT TO

WALTER, *by the door of the Oval Office. The letter opener is tight in his hand now.*

The door opens.

RICHMOND, *arms out, comes to embrace him, as he embraced him at the Press Conference.*

CUT TO

LUTHER *pulling up into the parking lot of the hospital, getting out, passing the parking lot attendant who is listening transfixed to a small radio.*

RADIO ANNOUNCER #1 (over)
In the greatest shock to the nation since the Kennedy assassination, President Alan Richmond's death has rocked —

LUTHER *has moved past now; we can't hear the radio anymore.*

CUT TO

HOSPITAL RECEPTION AREA.

LUTHER *enters. A number of people are present, all of them listening to a large radio, on the desk of the information clerk.*

RADIO ANNOUNCER #2 (over)
...Richmond died violently in the Oval Office and Walter Sullivan...

LUTHER *has moved past now; we can't hear the radio anymore.*

CUT TO

KATE'S HOSPITAL ROOM.

She dozes. LUTHER sits alongside in a chair.

Outside, the moon is high in the sky.

KATE blinks, half opens her eyes, sees LUTHER.

KATE

...you're still here...?

LUTHER

Haven't budged.

(she dozes again)

CUT TO

HOSPITAL LOUNGE.

A coffee machine in a lounge. Empty. But a TELEVISION SET IS PLAYING SOFTLY.

LUTHER enters, gets some coffee.

The TV is SHOWING the PRESS CONFERENCE RICHMOND held. As we watch, Walter Sullivan moves down toward the President and they embrace.

Now the press conference is over and we are LIVE AT THE FRONT OF the North Portico of the White House. A ton of reporters...

...and WALTER SULLIVAN in their midst, beckoning for quiet.

REPORTER #1

Mister Sullivan, have you no idea why the President took his own life?

LUTHER stops making coffee, looks at the screen.

WALTER SULLIVAN
(voice soft)

I know he's been feeling the pressure of office more than ever lately. We've talked about it a great deal.

REPORTER #2

But why would he stab himself?

> WALTER SULLIVAN
> *(sadly)*
> That's a question that will haunt me forever. Of course I tried to stop him —
> *(beat)*
> — Alan was like a son to me . . .

LUTHER smiles, takes his coffee, leaves the room as we —

CUT TO

KATE's HOSPITAL ROOM.

KATE sleeping. SETH stands there now. LUTHER enters with his coffee. Seth sees him and they both move to the door and confer silently —

— SETH indicates KATE.

LUTHER crosses his fingers.

SETH says something we can't make out.

LUTHER nods.

SETH glances a final time at KATE, then leaves them.

LUTHER moves to KATE, studies her face.

> KATE
> *(eyes still closed)*
> . . . was that Seth . . . ?

> LUTHER
> He was just checking in. When you're up to it, he said we might come over for dinner.

LUTHER arranges her sheets.

> KATE
> . . . you don't have to fuss . . .

> LUTHER
> You were forever catching colds.

She nods, drifts, and we —

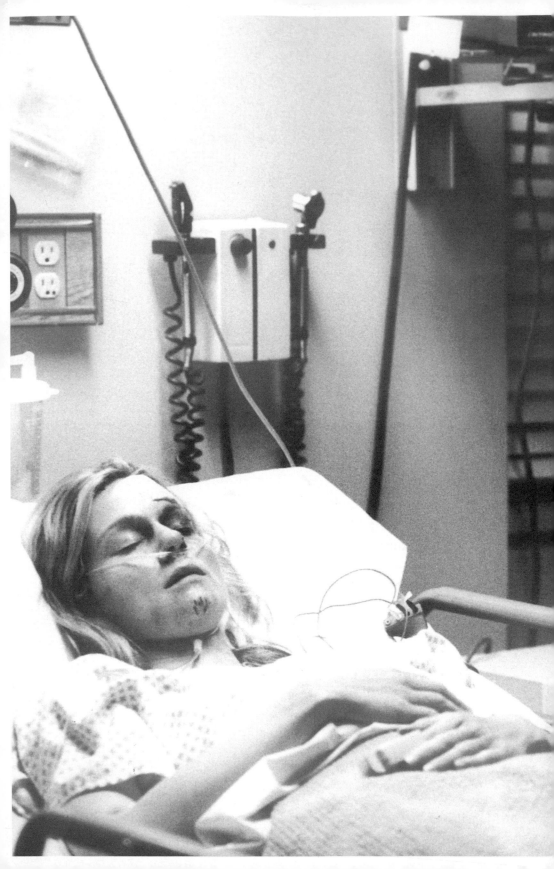

CUT TO

THE MOON

starting to fall out of the sky now.

LUTHER stands by the window, looking out. Soon, dawn. He stretches, crosses to her.

                         KATE
    ...am I going to be all right?...

                        LUTHER
                      (long pause)
        We'll be fine.

Kate nods, drifts.

LUTHER watches her.

Then he goes to his chair —

— reaches down —

— pulls out his sketchbook.

He turns the pages.

Drawings of KATE.

He turns to a new page.

Starts drawing her again.

He's really getting good.

HOLD ON LUTHER AND KATE

FINAL FADE OUT.